THE MAGICKAL YEAR

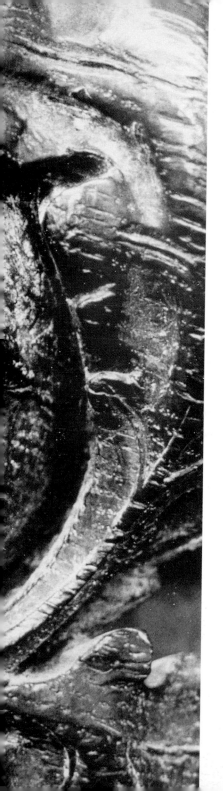

THE
MAGICKAL
YEAR

DIANA FERGUSON

SAMUEL WEISER, INC.
York Beach, Maine

A LABYRINTH BOOK

THE MAGICKAL YEAR

First published in the United States in 1996 by
Samuel Weiser, Inc.
P. O. Box 612
York Beach, ME 03910-0612

Library of Congress Cataloging-in-Publication Data
Ferguson, Diana.
    The magickal year / Diana Ferguson.
          p. cm.
        1. Magic. 2. Ritual. 3. Paganism. 4. Seasons--Mythology.
    I. Title.
    BF1623.R6F   1996
    133.4'3--dc20   96-973
    ISBN 0-87728-882-8   CIP

Printed in Italy

02 01 00 99 98 97 96
10 9 8 7 6 5 4 3 2 1

CONTENTS

TREMBLING THE WEB OF WYRD

No man is an Iland, intire of it selfe;
every man is a peece of the Continent,
a part of the maine ...

(*DEVOTIONS*, NO. XVIII, JOHN DONNE 1571?-1631)

I magine a spider's web, intricate as lace and so invisibly fine that, as they say in the old stories, it would pass seven times through the eye of a needle. See the skeins stretching between twigs, leaves and through the empty spaces in between. The tiniest movement of one of the skeins—caused by a breeze, an insect alighting, a leaf falling—sets the web quivering and sends vibrations rippling through to the furthest thread. So it is with magic. An act of magic reverberates through the invisible web of fate that connects all things, and affects the fortunes of humankind.

This "Web of Wyrd" is the mind-picture of the Anglo-Saxons. For them, "Wyrd"—from which we get our word "weird"—was Fate, and the workings of magic were known as "trembling the Web of Wyrd."

The idea of a network, force, or body linking all creation, so that a movement in one part affects the whole, is both as old as time and thoroughly modern. We find it in ancient man's belief in the World Soul that infuses all things and makes them one. We find it in the Jungian concept of the collective unconscious, that great ocean on which each of us floats—a separate personal unconscious—but which joins us all. We find it in the eternally shifting and flowing energy field into which we connect when we do creative visualization. We even find it in modern physics, in what is known as the Butterfly Effect—the "sensitive dependence on initial conditions" pictured as the fluttering of a butterfly on one side of the world which sets in motion a chain reaction culminating on the other side .

OPPOSITE: The tiniest movement of one of the threads will set this web a-quivering, and so it is with the workings of magic, as they send tremors through the Web of Fate.

OPPOSITE: This elaborate well headstone is an enduring testimony to the importance and sanctity of wells to our ancestors.

Magic is a "sympathetic" process: it operates on the basis of an affinity between things, and there are several forms. One kind of magic works by imitation, and is based on the principle that like produces like. So, for example, lighting the sacred flame in the form of a fire or a candle rekindles the great fire, the Sun, and causes him to return after the Winter Solstice. Alternatively, kindling the destructive fire in a purification ritual will symbolically "destroy" unwanted forces.

Another kind of sympathetic magic is based on the idea that a kind of *geist*, a life essence, permeates every part of a person. Even if a tiny portion of that person is separated from the whole, an invisible link is still maintained, and whatever happens to one will happen to the other. So, for example, "harming a hair" from someone's head will also harm that person. The connection was also extended to include objects that had been in close physical contact with an individual, such as, say, an arrow that had inflicted a wound. Cleaning the arrowhead, oiling it, and generally caring for it was the same as caring for the victim directly, and would therefore help the wound to heal more quickly.

As well as the magic that "puts out" in this way there is also the magic that "takes in." The person who partakes of the Communion bread and wine in order to absorb some of God's Holy Spirit is sharing in the same sacred activity as the hunter who eats the flesh and drinks the blood of the sacrificial animal in order to be one with the World Soul.

When our forebears engaged in communal acts of magic, they did so for the most basic of reasons—to survive. In a world ruled by forces beyond their control, they had a respect and reverence for Nature which we have largely lost. The rituals and ceremonies of their seasonal festivals were attempts to ensure the continuation of the eternal cycle of the seasons, so that crops, animals, and man might once again be renewed and revived. As they sought both to influence and to propitiate the divine powers of Nature, magic and religion combined in the great melting pot of pagan mystery.

Magic is with us still. When we touch wood, drink a toast "for luck," visualize something we want, or even make the sign of the cross to avert misfortune, we are remembering the old ways; we are sending ripples out into the great ocean of the Universe and drinking from the cup that washes back to our shore.

IN THE BEGINNING...
...GOD

THE MOON, THE SUN AND THE WHEEL OF FORTUNE

To see a World in a Grain of Sand,
And a Heaven in a Wild Flower,
Hold Infinity in the palm of your hand,
And Eternity in an hour.

(*AUGURIES OF INNOCENCE*, WILLIAM BLAKE, 1757-1827)

Once upon a time, long, long ago—perhaps as much as three and a half million years or more—an event occurred that was to set in motion a whole train of action that would eventually change the entire balance of life on this planet. A small, hairy, ape-like creature, who normally moved about on all fours, came down from his home in the trees, stretched himself into an upright position and, teetering unsteadily, took his first step on his two hind legs. Like a baby learning to walk, the creature practiced his new trick until he had mastered it. He learned other tricks, too, but it took him a while—another million years or so, when he discovered how to use pieces of stone as tools and weapons. Given another couple of million years of learning through play, he discovered how to make fire, and later to form implements and arms from bronze and iron.

All these were wonderful achievements, of course, but the most significant feat the ape-like infant learned to perform was to use the invisible power of thought. It was his superior ability to analyze, to reason, to imagine—and to name the objects around him with individual sounds so that he could communicate with others of his species—that finally gave him mastery over all other forms of life, even those that were superior to him in physical strength.

Ancient images still evoke powerful responses. In this modern painting by Gordon Wain, the Goddess wears "lunar" horns, while a Green Man emerges from the undergrowth.

The primitive infant who made such impressive progress through his formative years was, of course, the ancestor of modern man, known in the final stage of his development as *homo sapiens*.

WORLD OF WONDERS

Standing on his two strong legs, *homo sapiens* gazed about him in awe at the brave new world into which he had been born—and he wondered. The Earth on which he stood provided everything he needed, as if by magic: when he was hungry, there were animals that he could hunt, or edible plants that he could gather for food; when he was thirsty, there were streams and rivers whose waters he could drink. He knew when to sleep and to wake, for his natural rhythms were attuned to the coming of the darkness and the light. Light and warmth came when the great, blinding ball of fire that we now call the Sun appeared above the edge of the world; coolness and darkness came when it disappeared over the far horizon. In this darkness, however, appeared an equally marvelous marvel—a shimmering, silver orb now known as the Moon that spread a soft blanket of blue light over all the land.

The human infant was not yet clever enough to harness the power of the wonders which he saw around him: he could do little more than stand and stare. The natural phenomena which he could neither understand nor control were so transcendent, so beyond the scope of his puny reasoning, that he began to worship them. And so was born the concept of the divine—of an omnipotent being or beings who had the power to create or destroy, to control destiny. Over the millennia that followed, *homo sapiens* grew up. As his abilities, understanding, and way of life evolved, so too did his view of the divine.

MOTHER EARTH

In his attempt to make sense of the world in which he lived, early man invented identities for the powerful forces around him. In his deification of the Earth he had the perfect role model close at hand—Woman. Like the Earth, prehistoric woman seemed able—by some miraculous and unfathomable process—to bring forth life at will, as and when she chose. Full realization of the part played by men in conception did not take hold, some scholars believe, until just before the beginning of the Iron Age, about 3,500 years ago (the phallus as a male emblem had been in evidence well before this time, but had been offered in worship to the Goddess, rather than venerated in its own right). Woman's ability to produce another human being out of her belly was seen as the supreme act of magic. She was therefore to be revered and honored, for she was the possessor of the secret of life, which was denied to man.

On the walls of Les Trois Frères caves in France, a skin-clad hunter, half-human, half-animal, high-steps in sacred dance as he wounds a bison. This painting dates from around 14,000 B.C.

Having given birth to her baby, Woman was now the mother whose body provided food for her child, and who nurtured and protected it. In the same way, the Earth also fed and cared for her "children"—the human species—and so became personified as female and a mother. Just as Woman was the Mother of Man, the Earth was Mother of Mankind. She was the Great Mother, the Source of All Life—the Goddess.

The concept of the Goddess is extremely old—some say 25,000 years, some say more, which places her time of origin in the Paleolithic (Old Stone) Age. The ancient Romans had a name for her which we still use: they called her Gaia, Mother Earth who "gave birth to herself," bringing herself forth from the void of chaos that preceded the beginning of matter and time. Images of the Goddess, known as "Venus figurines" after the Roman goddess of love—made of stone or ivory in Europe, and clay in Egypt—have been found dating from as long ago as 25,000 B.C. In 7,000 B.C. the first shrines to her appeared in Jericho; by 3,000 B.C. her worship had spread throughout the known world, where she was represented in statues, shrines and writings.

ABOVE: A paleolithic celebration of motherhood: the Willendorf Venus, *a stone figurine from 25,000 B.C.*

RIGHT: Women under the influence of the Moon in a wood engraving of 1890. Woman's menstrual cycle, the changes in her body shape during pregnancy and afterwards, and her three ages as Virgin, Mother, and Crone, have all been linked with the waxing and waning of the Moon.

SISTER MOON

The Moon is another very ancient symbol of female divinity and power. Observations of the Moon revealed a mysterious, repetitive pattern of behavior. Whereas the Sun either "is" or "is not"—it always stays the same shape and is either risen or set—the Moon is in an endless state of becoming-waxing, waning, shrinking, renewing, ever in flux. Unlike the Sun, who operates in a linear way, having a clear-cut beginning and ending, the Moon works in an eternally recurring cycle, growing, declining, and growing once more. In a beautiful analogy, the Babylonians called her "the fruit that grows from itself."

This lunar pattern of waxing and waning echoed the very rhythms of life itself, a process intimately connected with the female, who was seen as the originator of life. Once a month, the Moon "died" only to be "reborn." Once a month, Woman bled but lived on; during pregnancy, her body swelled like the Full Moon, but after delivery it returned to its former shape as if starting all over again, like the New Moon. The Earth, in her alternating periods of fertility and decay, lived and died, and the Sea flowed and ebbed according to the waxing and waning of the Moon. All these images of the essential feminine—Earth, Woman, Moon, and Sea—melded together in the personality of the Goddess.

As well as contributing to this personality, the Moon also provided mankind with a powerful symbol of hope. Shining out of the blackness of the night sky, her cycle of death and rebirth was easy to observe. Since she could clearly be seen to die and live again, so might all living creatures—including man. The mystical continuum of life-death-life has exercised the human mind since the dim beginnings of religious thought, and has been expressed in various ways, from such visible manifestations as the death and rebirth of vegetation to abstract concepts such as reincarnation, resurrection, and immortality.

L'Influance
de la lune Sur la
teste des femmes

ABOVE: *An illustration from* The Saturday Magazine *published in London in 1834, showing "the Saxon idol" of the Moon. The circular, mirror-like disk which the figure proffers encompasses both Full and Crescent shapes.*

OPPOSITE, TOP: *A Crescent Moon which may be either Waxing, as Virgin, or waning, as Crone.*

OPPOSITE, BOTTOM: *A huge, almost-Full Moon still has a powerfully magic quality. The rounded form of the Full Moon suggests the Mother.*

TIME AND THE MOON

Although days could be measured by the Sun, the changing phases of the Moon provided Paleolithic (Old Stone Age) people with a means of measuring longer stretches of time. The importance of the Moon as a first clock is enshrined in language, in which the name for Moon also provides the words measurement, month, and menstruation. The English word month is connected with Moon; in Latin *mensis* means month and *mensura* is measurement, which also gives us the lunar-based menstrual cycle.

THE CIRCLE AND THE SPIRAL

In the modern Western world, we see life as a series of beginnings, middles, and endings. The geometric form representing this view is the line which, because of its very nature, has to start somewhere and stop somewhere else. The circle, however, depicts an older view of life, based on the rhythms of Nature that flow round and round in the eternally recurring cycle of death and regeneration. The circling spiral—that can be followed all the way in to the middle and all the way out again—has the same meaning, and is frequently found carved on stones at the entrances to prehistoric-burial mounds.

THE FACES OF THE GODDESS

The Goddess had a number of faces, acquired in her origins as both Earth and Moon. The Earth essentially has two phases: in the first, when vegetation is growing to feed man and beast, she is the life-giver; in her second phase, when vegetation is dying, she is the life-taker. What she takes back into herself, however, she will give birth to in the following season. By analogy with the Earth, the Goddess shows two corresponding faces, that of Creator and that of Destroyer. She is both the fertile Goddess of Love who creates life, and the Goddess of Death who destroys what she has created.

The Moon, however, has three faces, which correspond to the three ages of Woman. There is the Waxing Moon who is the Virgin, the Full Moon who is the Mother, and the Waning Moon who is the Crone. To these can be added a fourth phase, the Dark Moon, which represents the three days at the end of each lunar cycle when the Moon disappears entirely: this is the Crone at her oldest. Following the lunar model, the Goddess sometimes appears as a trinity known as the Triple Goddess, which may include all three "ages" of the Moon.

The terms "virgin" and "mother," in particular, need some brief explanation for their modern connotations cloud their meaning. Here, the Goddess is not virgin in that she has not had a man, but in that she does not need a man to produce offspring. Her chastity or lack of it is totally irrelevant to her ability to bear children, as it would have seemed for women before the concept of biological fatherhood arose. One meaning of the word "virgin" is "unmarried woman," and as Virgin the Goddess retains her autonomy and her separateness.

THE MOON GODDESS AND THE SEASONS		
LUNAR PHASE	**GODDESS**	**SEASON**
Waxing	Virgin	Spring
Full	Mother	Summer
Waning	Crone	Autumn
Dark	Crone	Winter

The Goddess as Mother can be equally misleading. Unlike the modern stereotype of the term, she is no self-sacrificing figure but one who revels in the full power of her womanhood and her sexuality. She is Woman in all the glory of her fertility.

The Virgin and Mother phases of the Moon correspond to the Earth's period of growth, to Spring and Summer; the Crone and Dark Moon phases are associated with the Earth's decline, and the seasons of Autumn and Winter.

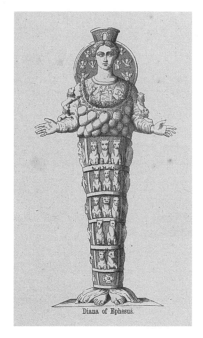

Diana of Ephesus.

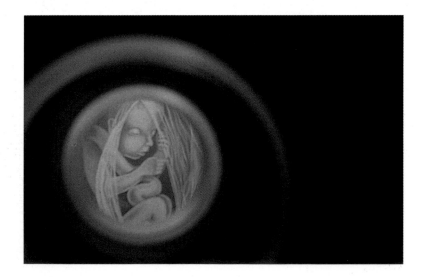

ABOVE: The Roman Moon Goddess Diana (Artemis in Greek) had three faces: Virgin Goddess, Mother of Animals, and Huntress (or Destroyer). At Ephesus, where her famous temple stood, she was worshipped as the Great Mother, whose many breasts nourished all living creatures.

LEFT: In esoteric belief, the Moon was the Gate of Birth who "sent" life into a woman's womb, where it could assume physical form. "Gate" was also a common metaphor for the female genitals, out of which life came.

THE IMAGE OF MAN

The personalities and names of the divine beings who ruled over the world of man constantly changed throughout the development of religion, and it is important to remember this when working through the mazes of ancient theologies. The Goddess, for example, originally based on the concept of fertile woman—Mother Earth—gradually acquired other attributes, and with them separate names, thus becoming not just one overall deity but a group of different deities.

The evolution of the male divinity happened in the opposite way. He began as a "child" of the Goddess whose presence was immanent in Nature—she was Nature itself—and he was an outward incarnation of her divinity. Gradually, however, he outgrew her and replaced her as an emanent God, who existed outside Nature, and from whom Nature issued.

This shift in the balance of power did not happen accidentally. It was a reflection of changes in human society for—contrary to the Biblical saying, "Man is made in the image of God"—God is more often made in the image of Man. Man's way of life and his relationship to the world around him is mirrored in the deities he creates. A battle-hardened, warrior race, for example, would hardly choose to worship the same kind of sensual fertility god as a peace-loving, agrarian community.

Changing ways of life brought with them new gods and goddesses. People who lived according to the Stone-Age tradition of harmony with the rhythms of Nature and whose central figure of worship was the Great Goddess had, by the Iron Age, been overcome by nomadic, warrior tribes, who brought with them their battle gods of sky and storm. To see how a particular people's way of life can color their view of the divine, one has only to compare the fertility deities of, say, ancient Asia Minor or pre-classical Greece with the pantheons of the warlike Teutons—in which goddesses are rare and not very prominent—and, to a lesser extent, of the Celts. While Celtic goddesses retained some of the old Earth – mother traits, Celtic gods were warriors, chieftains, and heroes.

Thus the process that began with Goddess ended with God—a god, moreover, who would not even allow his predecessor any credit. Yahweh,

Wielding his hammer, the Norse god Thor calls up a tempest of thunder and lightning.

God of the Judeo-Christian tradition which is most familiar to Western peoples—and who is drawn from the Babylonian model of the conqueror god Marduk—achieved his victory in the Garden "eastward of Eden" when he claimed for himself the key function of the Great Mother—the ability to bring forth life. In a biological role reversal Yahweh, the Father God, created Eve, the "Mother of All Living" and Goddess now reduced to human form. To emphasize her lowly status, not only was she born human, but she was also created after her husband Adam, from his rib, and was thus subordinate both to God and to Man.

The Christian male monotheism—child of Judaism and cousin of Islam—supplanted Eve with another version of the Goddess, the Virgin Mary, and turned the deities of the pagan pantheon into saints, at best, or demons, at worst.

The overthrow of the Goddess by the God runs parallel with mankind's gradual separation from Nature. In the beginning, the human species was as dependent on the Earth for its survival as a baby is on its mother; slowly, as scientific knowledge grew, people learned how to control and dominate the Earth, and broke the old symbiotic bond—rather like a boy child who rejects his mother and the feminine qualities for which she stands as the only way to achieve a personal, masculine identity. This disregard for the Earth and Nature and for the interdependence of all life is something for which we may yet pay dearly, not only in environmental damage but in a loss of contact with our innermost selves. The doctrine of separateness from and mastery over the Earth was expressed most succinctly way back at the beginning of the Old Testament by patriarch-chieftain Yahweh when he gave Adam and Eve his message of domination—a message that has thundered out across the centuries ever since:

Be fruitful, and multiply,
and replenish the earth, and subdue it: and have dominion over the
fish of the sea, and over the fowl of the air, and over every living
thing that moveth upon the earth.

(*GENESIS*, CHAPTER 1, VERSE 28)

OPPOSITE: This woodcut of c. 1510 shows God producing Eve out of the side of a slumbering Adam, and the final expulsion of the pair from the Garden by an angel armed with a flaming sword. Taken as metaphor, the story tells of the subjugation of the Goddess, and of mankind's split from Nature.

NATURE SPIRIT

Going back to the beginning, before the rise of the Father God, the earliest form of male deity was probably the Horned God. This mythic figure was born of the tradition of Stone Age hunting communities who, in the bitter cold of successive ice ages when plant life was minimal, had to depend largely on wild animals for food. He was, in a way, the "son" of the Goddess in that he symbolized one aspect of Nature, one part of the Whole—the part that was animal. Although he still bore the Goddess' emblem—a pair of horns that mimicked her lunar crescent—he had created for himself his own small, separate identity. His prototype may be seen in 16,000-year-old cave paintings in France and Spain, which depict a dancing, bison-headed or goat-horned figure, or a man wearing antlers and a deer skin. As an expression of

In this painting by Gordon Wain, the Teutonic god Woden has been depicted as a horned god, an early form of the male deity. Woden's role as World Magician links him to the animal shamans of the prehistoric cave paintings.

the soul of Nature yet with some of the appearance of a man, this horned figure fused hunter and hunted in a mystical union of human and divine. Later, in the Neolithic (New Stone) Age as the glaciers melted and the climate grew warmer, people no longer had to follow the herds but were able to settle and cultivate crops. Now a new incarnation of the "son of Nature" evolved. This was the Green Man, who was the spirit of vegetation. As agriculture developed and mankind moved into the Bronze Age, the Green Man was thought to be embodied in such crops as corn or vines, and had an intimate connection with the fertility of the soil. During the Earth's dormant period, he lay in her "womb" in the form of seeds and roots hidden beneath the soil; when her growing season began, he was "born" from her womb in the form of new plants. These new plants would, in their turn, wither and die, leaving their roots in the soil or dropping their seeds to provide next season's crop, thus establishing an endless cycle of life, death, and regeneration.

The Green Man in a Christian house of worship. His unnerving face peers down from a ceiling in Norwich Cathedral, England.

Being both plant and provider of seed, the Green Man had a dual role: when he grew out of the Earth as a plant, he was her "son," but when he made the Earth fertile with his seeds, he was her "lover." In this seeming paradox we see the origin of the great, central myth of the old Bronze Age religions of the Mediterranean and Near East, namely, that of the Goddess and her son-lover, who lives, dies, and is reborn.

24

OPPOSITE, TOP: The worship of the Sun is common to many cultures. In a circular temple, worshippers bow down before a gigantic effigy of the solar deity.

OPPOSITE, BOTTOM: A statue of Surya, the ancient Indian Sun god.

BELOW: Here, a Hopi from New Mexico appears in the costume of the solar god.

THE CONQUERING HERO

The Assyrian came down like the wolf on the fold …
(*THE DESTRUCTION OF SENNACHERIB*, LORD BYRON, 1788-1824)

The third and final face of the male deity that is relevant to the pagan festivals of the year is that of the Sun God. The Sun is the day-time counterpart of the night-time Moon, and has been worshipped for thousands of years. In one Egyptian myth, the goddess Nut gave birth to both the Sun and the Moon. The solar god had particular appeal, however, for the warlike people of the Iron Age, who saw him as the triumphant God of Light who had come to banish the darkness. He represented their ideal—the warrior hero. One Roman name for the solar god, *Sol Invictus* or "the unconquered Sun" perfectly expresses this image.

The Sun's nature makes it inevitable that he will behave in this way. Unlike the changeable and flexible Moon, he either "is" or "isn't" and therefore cannot be accommodating: the only way he can exist is by overcoming. Such a vision has a polarizing effect, however: on the one hand there is the Moon, perceived as female, with her "feminine" qualities of mystery, imagination, and receptivity; on the other hand, there is the Sun, seen as male, with his "masculine" attributes of clarity, reason, and initiative.

Historically the image of an invincible sun god is a product of the Indo-European and Semitic traditions. Around 4,300 B.C. the first wave of invasions by peoples known as "Indo-Europeans" or "Aryans" began, and progressively swept westwards across Europe, south into the Middle East, and east towards India. These warlike nomads probably originated on the steppes between the Dnieper and Volga rivers north of the Black Sea, and brought with them an ethos that was completely different from the peaceful, holistic vision of the Stone Age. Their beliefs were solar-oriented, not lunar; they worshipped male sky gods of thunder, lightning and fire, glorified the warrior with his battle-ax and blade, and had a culture with an hierarchical, patriarchal base. Not for them the eternally revolving cycles of Nature, but a doctrine of opposites and finality, struggle and victory.

About 500 years earlier, these Indo-Europeans had domesticated the horse and, equipped with this newly invented means of transport, were able to move across the land at lightning speed. The sight of men on horseback for the first time must have inspired the most enormous terror (and may have been the model for the Greek centaur, half-man, half-horse); such apocalyptic, horse-riding hordes are perhaps what one Sumerian observer was describing when he wrote in 2,100 B.C. of "a host whose onslaught was like a hurricane, a people who had never known a city." (Quoted in *Prehistoric India*, Stuart Piggot). It was fear of these invaders, and the need for defense, which produced the hill fort and the city wall.

At around the same time as the Indo-Europeans began their invasions, Semitic tribes were moving northwards into Mesopotamia and Canaan (roughly modern Iraq and Palestine) from the Syrian and Arabian deserts, bringing with them a world view similar to that of the Indo-Europeans. Like them, the Semites also worshipped sky gods who dwelt in the clouds and on mountain-tops, and they saw themselves as separate from Nature, which they viewed as a hostile force to be subdued if human life was to survive. The impact of these invasions which brought so much turbulence to the Bronze Age cannot be overestimated. As the newcomers overran the Old World, they imposed different values on the ancient culture of the Mother Goddess— values which have survived well into modern times. By the beginning of the Iron Age, the ethos of the warrior chieftain, combined with the new understanding of biological paternity, had prepared the perfect setting for the entrance of an omnipotent and emanent father god, who created all life but chose to control it from a position somewhere outside physical creation. In the images of new God and old Goddess, we see the two broad, contrasting bands of faith and thought—Iron Age and Stone Age, male and female, sky and earth, spirit and body, intellect and feeling, doing and being.

THE AGE OF STONE

PALEOLITHIC (OLD STONE) AGE (c. 2,500,000-7,000 B.C)
The Great Mother, the Horned God and the Hunter-Gatherer

- homo habilis (handy man) makes first stone tools
  c. 2,500,000 B.C.
- homo erectus (upright man) appears
  c. 1,500,000 B.C.
- homo erectus makes fire c. 600,000 B.C.
- homo sapiens neanderthalensis (Neanderthal man)
  appears c. 100,000 B.C.
- Neanderthal man buries dead c. 75,000 B.C.
- homo sapiens sapiens (thinking man, modern
  man) appears c. 50,000 B.C.
- first cave paintings c. 20,000 B.C.

NEOLITHIC (NEW STONE) AGE (c. 9,000-5,000 B.C.)
The Herder-Grower and the Villager

- animals domesticated and small-scale cultivation
  begins c. 9,000 B.C. in western Asia, c. 7,000 B.C. in
  Balkans and Greece

THE AGE OF BRONZE

(c. 6,000-1,200 B.C.in Middle East, 2,000-500 B.C. in Europe)
The Great Mother, the Green Man, the Farmer and the Citizen

- experiments with copper and gold c. 6,000 B.C.
- Indo-Europeans (Ayrans) domesticate horse c. 5,000 B.C.
- irrigation systems developed in Mesopotamia (modern
  Iraq) c. 5,500 B.C.
- agrarian settlements in Nile Valley by c. 5,000 B.C.
- First plow used in Mesopotamia c. 4,500 B.C.
- first wave of Indo-European invaders from north of Black
  Sea into Europe c. 4,300 B.C. (later invading Middle East
  and India)
- Semitic tribes begin migrating from Syro-Arabian desert to
  Mesopotamia and Canaan c. 4,000 B.C.
- rise of Sumerian civilization in Mesopotamia c. 3,500 B.C.
  Sumerians produce bronze, an alloy of copper and tin
  (perhaps first invented in Thailand), build cities from brick,
  and invent the wheel
- rise of Minoan civilization of Crete c. 3,000 B.C.
- Sumerians develop picture writing (cuneiform)
  c. 3,250 B.C.
- rise of Indus Valley civilization c. 2,600 B.C.
- Old Kingdom of Egypt reaches height of power
  c. 2,600 B.C.
- bronze-making spreads across Europe c. 2,500 B.C.
- Middle Kingdom of Egypt c. 2,200-1,800 B.C.
- Babylonian empire established c. 1,750 B.C.
- rise of first Greek Mycenaen civilization c. 1,600 B.C.
- New Kingdom of Egypt and peak of Egyptian civilization
  under pharaohs c. 1,580 B.C.
- first experiments with iron-smelting in Middle East
  c. 1,500 B.C.

THE AGE OF IRON (c. 1,250 B.C.)
The Father God, the Conquering Sun and the Warrior

- discovery of iron smelting technique in Middle East
  c. 1,500 B.C.
- rise of Judaism in Palestine c. 1,200 B.C
- first known Celtic territory in central Europe
  c. 1,200 B.C.
- iron replaces bronze in Middle East and Greece
  c. 1,000 B.C.
- use of iron spreads across Europe, and Celts become
  expert iron-workers c. 800 B.C.
- founding of the city of Rome 753 B.C.
- Celts arrive in Spain and Portugal c. 600 B.C. and spread
  into other parts of Europe including Britain and Ireland
- founding of Persian empire 550 B.C.
- Greeks under Alexander the Great conquer
  Egypt 332 B.C.
- Romans conquer Greece c. 146 B.C.
- death of Jesus Christ c. A.D. 30 and rise of Christianity
- Roman Empire stretches from Britain to Mesopotamia
  under emperor Trajan A.D. 52-117
- death of Mohammed A.D. 632 and spread of Islam
- Christianity adopted as official religion of Roman Empire
  by Emperor Constantine A.D. 312

*The slaying of the bull of the Babylonian goddess Ishtar. The
sacred bull embodying a god was a widespread Bronze Age
myth. When representing the Goddess's consort, the bull was
often sacrificed to her.*

With no beginning or ending, the wheel symbolizes the recurring cycle of existence. Here, wheels adorn the Black Pagoda at Konarak, India.

THE WHEEL OF FORTUNE

The life, death, and rebirth of the Goddess and the God in his various incarnations were cycles of crucial importance to mankind, for on them depended the survival of the species. The respective cycles can be combined in the image of a giant wheel, intersected by joints which are the key turning points in the year for the Earth, Moon, Vegetation God, and Sun.

It was essential that this wheel keep turning for it was truly mankind's Wheel of Fortune: if the Earth failed to complete her circular journey through death to renewal, if the Sun failed to return bringing back light and warmth, man was doomed. A very special force was therefore needed to propel the wheel and maintain its perpetual motion—that force was Magic. At each of the joints or "hinges" of the year, people held festivals in which magic rituals and ceremonies generated sufficient energy to rotate the wheel into its next phase.

Depending on the culture to which they belonged and the focus of that culture, two main cycles of festivals developed: one marked the passage of the Sun, while the other was linked to changes in the seasons, based on the lunar model. The four solar festivals were:

- *Winter Solstice* on December 21, the shortest day of the year, after which the Sun is "reborn"
- *Spring Equinox* on March 21, when day and night are equal
- *Summer Solstice* on June 21, the longest day, after which the Sun dies
- *Autumn Equinox* on September 23, when night equals day.

In this solar calendar, the two most important feasts are the Solstices which divide the year in half, and may be likened to midnight and midday, which divide the day and mark the lowest and highest points of the Sun's daily journey.

The festivals of the lunar, seasonal calendar have Celtic names, which is why it is often known as the Celtic calendar. They are:
- *Samhain or Halloween* on October 31, which is the start of Winter, and equates to the Dark Moon
- *Imbolc or Candlemas* on February 1, the first day of Spring, equivalent to the Waxing Moon

• *Beltane or May Day* on May 1, the beginning of Summer, and the Full Moon
• *Lughnasadh or Lammas* on August 1, which is the start of Autumn, and the Waning Moon.

In this cycle the two main festivals are Samhain and Beltane, which divide the year into Winter and Summer halves, *Geimredh* and *Samradh* respectively. These halves were again subdivided into quarters by Imbolc and Lughnasadh, the Winter quarters being *Geimradh* (again) and Earrach, the Summer quarters being *Samradh* (again) and *Foghamhar*.

As in Jewish practice, the Celts measured their days from their dusks—in other words, a day ran from evening to evening rather than midnight to midnight. Consequently, Celtic festivals began on what we would call the eve of the day, not on the day itself. This method of calculation makes sense when one remembers that the Moon, Queen of the Night, gave man his first means of measuring time.

Following the pattern of calculating days from evenings, Samhain, the beginning of the darkness of Winter, is also thought to have been the beginning of the Celtic year. Samhain, then, may be likened to dusk when the Moon appears and the Celtic day begins, and Beltane to dawn halfway through the Celtic day when the Moon fades.

This apparently curious analogy is hard for modern minds to grasp, as centuries of solar-oriented days make "lunar days" completely foreign to us.

Although Moon and Sun provide the basis for the two cycles of festivals, the cycles are by no means mutually exclusive. There is considerable overlap between the two as, over the centuries, different races and cultures have mixed with each other, adding their own sacred customs into the melting pot of pagan tradition. The Celts, for example, were originally herdspeople rather than farmers, so it seems that the significance of their festivals would originally have been connected with major points in the pastoral year, yet later they came to have associations with plant fertility or even the Sun. Conversely, a primarily solar feast may also have links with the growth of vegetation.

Christianity gradually replaced the old religions, but it did not banish the pagan festivals. In some cases, these celebrations were so much a part of popular culture that it would have been extremely difficult to abolish them. So, instead of challenging the existing traditions, the Church used the clever expedient of renaming and adapting the old festivals to the Christian story. In this way, for example, the old Winter Solstice feast which was the birthday of the infant Sun became the birthday of Jesus.

Along with the dates of the festivals, Christianity also absorbed much of the religious mystery and symbolism of its pagan forebears. The details of, for example, the Nativity, the Annunciation when Mary learns of her pregnancy, the son born to a virgin at midwinter and who dies on a wooden Cross and is resurrected at Easter, as well as the relationship of the Mother of God to the God the Father and God the Son, all have antecedents in the grand pagan archetypes of western Asia and the Mediterranean. The Christianity that grew from the seed of Judaism has its roots in the deep, rich soil of Sumeria, Babylon, Persia, and Greece, and this can be seen not only in the timing of Christian festivals but also in the fundamental concepts of this comparatively young religion.

THE SOLAR CYCLE

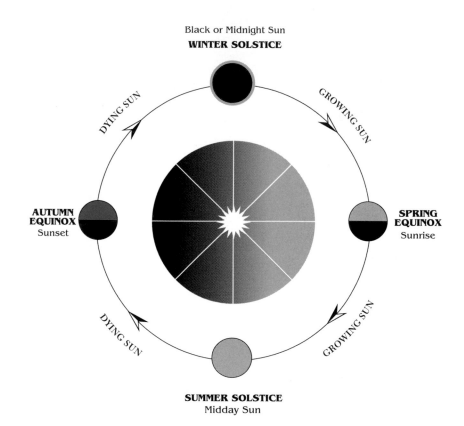

Black or Midnight Sun
WINTER SOLSTICE

GROWING SUN

DYING SUN

AUTUMN EQUINOX
Sunset

SPRING EQUINOX
Sunrise

DYING SUN

GROWING SUN

SUMMER SOLSTICE
Midday Sun

NEW FOR OLD

There have been other ways of dividing up the year, so that some of the festivals we now celebrate were once held on different dates, close by—which can sometimes lead to confusion.

All early calendars, except for the Egyptian, had a lunar structure. Around 46 B.C., the Roman emperor Julius Caesar introduced a calendar based on a

calculation of the solar year at 365¼ days. In the Julian Calendar, the missing day was "added on" every four years. But Caesar had slightly overestimated in his calculation: as the years passed there was a gradual build-up of extra days in his calendar, so that it synchronized less and less with the true solar year. In 1582, Pope Gregory XIII decided to set things to right by replacing the "Old Style" Julian Calendar with his "New Style" Gregorian Calendar, which adjusted the error by

THE LUNAR CYCLE

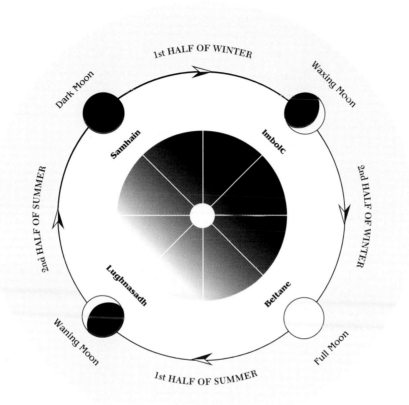

eliminating a number of days.

This is the calendar we now use, but it was not readily adopted everywhere. Resolutely Protestant Britain and her colonies held out against this "Popish" nonsense for another 170 years, by which time the discrepancy between calendar and solar year amounted to eleven days. To get back on track, in 1752 the calendar of the English-speaking world finally lost these superfluous days, with September 2 being immediately followed by September 14, an outrage that led to riots among the population. Imperial Russia showed similar reluctance and did not adopt the New Style calendar until the October Revolution of 1917. As a result, this historic event which, under the old system, erupted on October 25 suddenly "time-traveled" forward to November 7, its modern commemoration date.

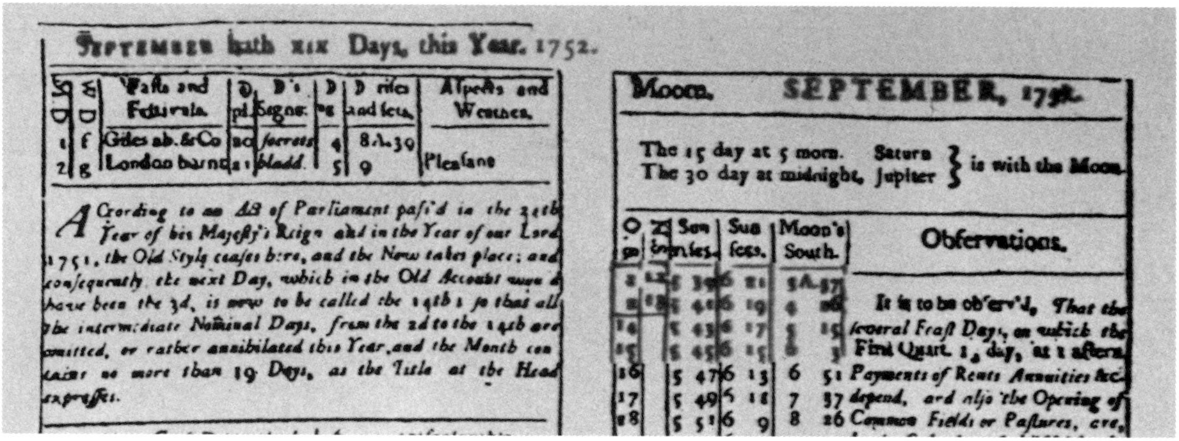
SEPTEMBER hath XIX Days, this Year. 1752.

Fasts and Festivals
Giles ab. & Co
London burnt
Pleasant

According to an Act of Parliament pass'd in the 24th Year of his Majesty's Reign and in the Year of our Lord 1751, the Old Style ceases here, and the New takes place; and consequently the next Day, which in the Old Account would have been the 3d, is now to be called the 14th; so that all the intermediate Nominal Days, from the 2d to the 14th are omitted, or rather annihilated this Year, and the Month contains no more than 19 Days, as the Title at the Head expresses.

Moon. SEPTEMBER, 1752.

The 15 day at 5 morn. Saturn } is with the Moon.
The 30 day at midnight. Jupiter }

Sun rises. Sun sets. Moon's South. Observations.

It is to be observ'd, That the several Feast Days, on which the First Quart. 1 day, at 1 aftern. Payments of Rents Annuities &c. depend, and also the Opening of Common Fields or Pastures, etc.

What all this means for the festivals of the pagan year is that, if one links them to specific dates rather than seasonal bands of time, they might not have quite the flavor one expects. In Western Europe Yuletide snow, for example, is more likely to fall on 6 January, which was Christmas Day in the Old Style tradition, than on the New Style December 25. May blossom may not be much in evidence on May 1, May Day New Style, but will be frothing joyously by May 13, May Day Old Style.

New Year is an even more movable feast. As explained earlier, the Celts probably celebrated this at the end of October, while in earlier Christian times the New Year began variously on Christmas Day, March 1, March 25—which is known as Lady Day and was New Year's Day Old Style—and even Easter Day. In ancient Egypt, the New Year was initiated on July 20 by the rise of the Dog Star, Sirius, symbol of the goddess Isis, which signaled the rise of the Nile's flood waters—the goddess's tears that would bring back her dead lover, Osiris. In Sumerian and Babylonian tradition, the New Year fell at the beginning of Spring, when the goddess Inanna or Ishtar lay with her lover Dumuzi or Tammuz in a sacred union that assured the fecundity of the Earth. Thus the date of the New Year varies from one culture to another depending on what constitutes the most significant turning point in the year for a particular people, whether it be the start of the Sun's ascendancy or the appearance of new plant life. In a way, as one moves through the solar and lunar calendars, each festival—especially such important ones as Samhain and Beltane and the solstices—is a New Year, a change from one major order to another, a new Creation.

A Year and a Day

But how many merry monthes be in the yeare?
There are thirteen, I say;
The mid-summer moon is the merryest of all,
Next to the merry month of May.

(*The Ballad of Robin and the Curtal Friar*)

The Moon and the Sun once divided up the year in more even fashion. The year itself was solar: it lasted 365 days, the length of the annual course of the Sun. The months, however, related to the Moon, and were based on the lunar, and classic menstrual, cycle of 28 days. Divide the 365-day Sun year by one 28-day Moon month, and you have 13 months with one day over—the "year and a day" still remembered in legend and story.

In druidic belief, each of these months was linked to a particular tree or plant. These were the Tree Months, each tree name also being that of one of the letters in the Tree Alphabet, the ancient ABC or Beth-Luis-Nuin.

THE TREE MONTHS

BETH (BIRCH)
    December 24 - January 20
LUIS (ROWAN)
    January 21 - February 17
NUIN (ASH)
    February 18 - March 17
FEARN (ALDER)
    March 18 - April 14
SAILLE (WILLOW)
    April 15 - May 12
HUATH (HAWTHORN)
    May 13 - June 9
DUIR (OAK)
    June 10 - July 7
TINNE (HOLLY)
    July 8 - August 4
COLL (HAZEL)
    August 5 - September 1
MUIN (VINE)
    September 2 - September 29
GORT (IVY)
    September 30 - October 27
PEITH (DWARF ELDER) OR
    NGETAL (REED)
    October 28 - November 24
RUIS (ELDER)
    November 25 - December 22
EXTRA DAY
    December 23

THE NEW MOON

Our word calendar comes from the Latin calendae, the first day of each month, when the appearance of the New Moon was solemnly proclaimed in ancient Rome.

THE DAYS OF THE WEEK

Everywhere in our language, our phrases ("in a nutshell," "I wouldn't harm a hair of your head"), our stories, our view of the world, reveal traces of our magical ways and of the deities we once worshipped. In the names we have given to the days of the week, we still honor the old gods and goddesses:

Sunday is the Sun's Day.
Monday is the Moon's Day.
Tuesday is the Day of Tiw or Tyr, Anglo-Saxon and Norse god of war.
Wednesday is Woden's Day, sacred to Woden or Odin, Anglo-Saxon and Norse father god and magician.
Thursday is Thor's Day, dedicated to the Norse storm god of thunder and lightning.
Friday is Freya's Day, the special day of Freya or Frigg, the Norse goddess of love.
Saturday is the Day of Saturn, the Roman Lord of Death, whose Greek name was Cronos. Saturn was also the Sun of Night, representing the Sun at his lowest ebb in Midwinter before he was reborn at the Winter Solstice—and on Sunday.

CHAPTER 2

THE DIVINE CHILD
DECEMBER 21: WINTER SOLSTICE;
CHRISTMAS AND NEW YEAR

The darkest hour is before the dawn.
(SEVENTEENTH-CENTURY PROVERB)

Whenever we place a star or an angel on top of a Christmas tree, set up a model Nativity scene complete with manger and adoring shepherds, light Yule candles, or sing carols, we are celebrating the birth of the Divine Child born in the depths of winter. Christians call him Jesus, but others in Mediterranean lands knew him as Apollo, Dionysus, Osiris, Adonis, Attis, Mithras, as well as other names, while in the far north the Norseman called him Frey or Balder.

Christmas Day, December 25, was the old date of the Winter Solstice (which now falls on December 21). In the solar calendar, this solstice is the year's "midnight." Although the world may seem very dark and bleak, it is a time for great hope and rejoicing for the Sun is due to be reborn. Before the solstice, he is at its weakest, and the solstice itself is the shortest day of the year; but then he is born again, and begins his growth from infancy to the full manhood he will achieve at the Summer Solstice. Such a momentous turning point inevitably inspired celebration and the Winter Solstice is a long-standing and widely observed time for joyful acknowledgment of the birth of the new Sun and Savior God under his myriad names—including that of Jesus.

In early Christian tradition, Christmas Day was once celebrated as the first day of the New Year, and in fact the significance and customs of New Year, which now falls six days later, are so inextricably bound up with those of Christmas that it is best to treat the two feasts as one and the same.

ABOVE AND RIGHT: Much traditional Yuletide imagery—the divine child born at Midwinter, the manger as crib, the ass and the ox, and the Christmas gift-bringer—is rich in pagan symbolism.

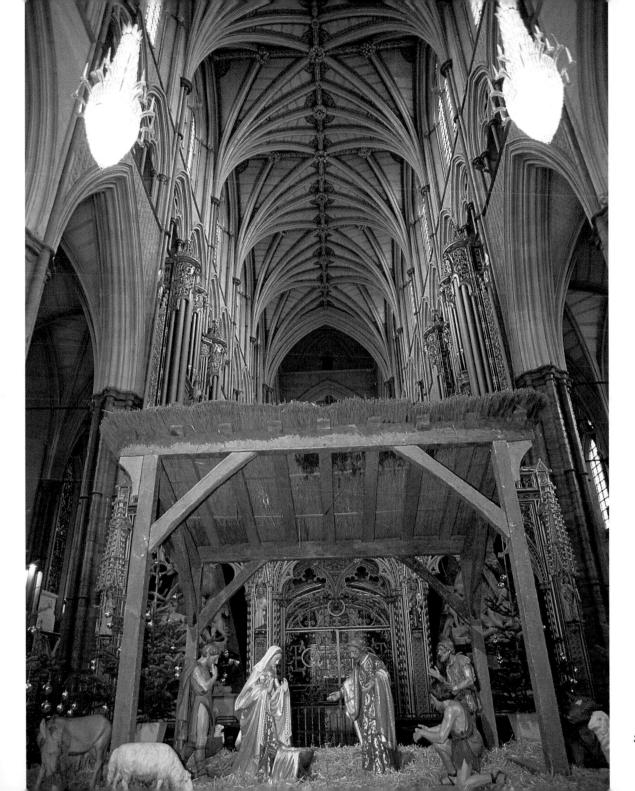

THE BABY IN THE BASKET

And there were in the same country shepherds abiding in the field, keeping watch over their flock by night. And, lo, the angel of the Lord came upon them, and the glory of the Lord shone round about them: and they were sore afraid. And the angel said unto them, Fear not: for, behold, I bring you good tidings of

great joy, which shall be to all people. For unto you is born this day in the city of David a Savior, which is Christ the Lord. And this shall be a sign unto you: Ye shall find the babe wrapped in swaddling clothes, lying in a manger. And suddenly there was with the angel a multitude of the heavenly host praising God, and saying, Glory to God in the highest, and on earth peace, good will toward men.

(ST. LUKE, CHAPTER 2, VERSES 8-14)

The Divine Child lying in the manger being adored by shepherds is a familiar feature of the Christmas tableau, but it also has echoes of the nativity scenes of the Roman god Mithra and the ancient Greeks' Dionysus.

Mithra's miraculous birth from the Mother Rock was observed by nearby shepherds, who came with their flocks to worship him. In the Eleusinian (Dionysus as Corn God) Mysteries, on which the Christian ones were based, the rebirth of Eleusis was celebrated. Priests dressed as shepherds carried in the Divine Child seated in a *liknon*, or harvest basket, to be worshipped by the company. The liknon was used not only as a winnowing fan, but as a manger and cradle, and "the Baby in the Basket" was called *Liknites*. Thus, the infant who was the life-spirit of the corn that would feed mankind (and whose body would later be eaten in the form of bread, as in the Christian Eucharist), was symbolically cradled in a basket for seed corn.

Similarly, in Celtic myth the infant Llew Llaw Gyffes skims over the water in a coracle made of weed and sedge—yet another baby in a basket, like Moses caught up among the bulrushes.

DEATH AND REBIRTH

The English word Yule is connected with *Giuli*, the Anglo-Saxon name for December, and there is also a possible link with the Anglo-Saxon word *hwéol*, meaning wheel—in other words, the wheel of the year that has completed its revolution at this time. In Gaelic the name for December was *An Mios marbh*, meaning the dead month and in Welsh it was *Rhagfyr*, or the month of preparation.

NAMING THE DAY

Because of changes in the calendar, there is confusion about the dating of Christmas day. In the Old Style Julian calendar it was deemed to be January 6 and is still observed on that day in the Christian Orthodox churches. Since the loss of eleven days in the calendar with the introduction of the Gregorian calendar it has been celebrated on December 25 in Western Europe and countries which were in its sphere of influence.

Both dates have pagan significance: January 6 is the date, recorded in fourth-century Egypt, when Aion, a composite of the god Osiris, was born to Kore, "the Maiden"—another personification of the ancient Egyptian goddess Isis—and December 25 was the birthday of the god Mithra, celebrated in ancient Rome as *Dies Natalis Solis Invictus*, meaning Birthday of the Unconquered Sun. Mithra originated from the Persian Mitra, whose name is first mentioned around 1,400 B.C. He was the embodiment of Light itself and, like the Greek sun god Apollo, rode a fiery chariot across the sky. He achieved preeminence in the Hellenistic period of Greek civilization, which lasted from 323 to 27 B.C. In Roman times, Mithraism was the chief rival to Christianity, exceeding it in popularity and holding sway in both Asia and in Europe, where it reached as far north as Scotland.

Although a pagan religion, Mithraism was patriarchal, like Christianity. In the fourth century A.D.—in an attempt to oust the competition—the Church claimed the birthdate of this god of Persian patriarchy for its own. According to one St. Chrysostom, the choice of December 25 as the birthday of "the Sun of Righteousness" was justifiable because "while the heathen were busied with their profane rites, the Christians might perform their holy ones without disturbance."

Christ's birthdate was decided in the 4th century A.D., and was based on that of the Persian god Mithra, here watched by a horned Moon and a Sun. In Mithraic myth, all living creatures were the progeny of a sacred bull, whose sacrificial blood was fructified by the Moon.

THE STAR OF WONDER

Now when Jesus was born in Bethlehem of Judea in the days of Herod the king, behold, there came wise men from the east to Jerusalem, saying, Where is he that is born King of the Jews? for we have seen his star in the east, and come to worship him … and, lo, the star, which they saw in the east, went before them, till it came and stood over where the young child was. When they saw the star, they rejoiced with exceeding great joy.
(St. Matthew, chapter 2, verses 1-2, 9)

The quintessence of Christmas—an evergreen, fairy tree, sparkling with flame, be-jewelled with "fruits," and topped with a star of promise, shines out of the darkness.

The Guiding Light that led the three wise men to the stable is an emblem of profound significance. *Stella Maris*, Latin for the Star of the Sea, was another name for the Goddess in several manifestations, while the Evening Star is identified with the goddess Venus.

The star is also an obvious symbol of hope, a beacon of light shining out of surrounding darkness and is found in many other traditions. Like the "star of wonder" of Christian legend, the rise of the Dog Star Sirius over the horizon signaled the beginning of the flooding of the Nile, which was the flood of tears wept by the goddess Isis that would bring back her lover Osiris to life. A similar good omen was watched for at the festival of Dionysus in Thrace. If a bright light shone in the sky, it promised an abundant harvest; if the sky remained dark, however, it was a warning that the harvest would be poor.

The burning of the Yule log in the Christmas fire was an important ritual to ensure good luck in the coming year.

THE SACRED FLAME

Kindle the Christmas brand, and then
Till sunneset let it burne;
Which quencht, then lay it up agen,
Till Christmas next returne.
Part must be kept, wherewith to teend
The Christmas log next yeare;
And where 'tis safely kept, the fiend
Can do no mischief there.

Fire has always played an important part at this crucial turning point in the solar calendar, the birth of the new Sun. If the Sun is the very embodiment of the divine, then fire—made in his image—becomes one of the most potent agents of magic, and a mystical medium of worship. Without the heat and light of the Sun there can be no life, so fire, his representative on Earth, is seen as a life-giving force—a "light to lighten the darkness."

Fire effects its magic in more than one way. In the flames is the energizing force of the divine Sun spreading his blessed rays on all living things; the flames also work as a purifying agent to destroy evil forces, for there are few substances that can escape their ravening, all-consuming power. At the same time, the wood being burnt embodies the God of Vegetation and his power to fertilize the Earth.

Such was the power of fire that it played an important part at many pagan festivals throughout the year, when great bonfires (from the Anglo-Saxon *banefyre*, literally bone-fire, or fires made from bones) would be set ablaze on the hilltops, like the great Jul bonfires that pierced the blackness of the Norse midwinter sky. The fires of this winter festival were a solemn ritual to prepare the way for the birth of the Divine Child, and to help him gain in strength so that the cycle of life might continue.

Smaller sacred fires were also lit on the domestic hearth at Midwinter, involving a special piece of wood known as the Yule Log. Depending on the locality, different rites accompanied the bringing in of this sacred log. First, on Christmas Eve, a suitable tree had to be found—say, an oak or a fruit tree—and a stout log, as large as possible, cut and ceremonially carried home. In some cases, a massive, gnarled oak root might be chosen. The log was then placed on the old fire, and hailed with music and song, or perhaps with a special incantation, such as, "Goodly be thy birth." Once the log was alight, the fire had to be maintained until New Year.

The log itself, as well as the fire it fed, was venerated. Because the log symbolized the vegetation deity, the Green Man, its ashes had magical, fertilizing powers. They might be scattered on the soil, like sacred seed, to make the Earth bear fruit—a custom that links in with the Hindu belief that ashes are the seed of the fire god Agni, from which new life springs. Alternatively, an unburned part of the log might be used to fashion a plow to fertilize the real seed in the soil, or kept under the bed until Twelfth Night to make poultry thrive.

LOOKING FOR A LIGHT

In the days of tinder-boxes, it was considered very unlucky, in the north of England, to let the fire go out between Christmas Eve and New Year's Day. Anyone asking a neighbor for a light would be refused. During the Calends, the first day of each Roman month, the citizens of Rome also refused to "give away fire," as if the giving away of the sacred flame was like giving away good fortune.

OPPOSITE: Yule candles are another way of calling on the mystical power of fire in the lightless depths of winter. Magical rituals using candles further enhanced their benign influence.

Keeping a piece of the Yule log during the year ensured plentiful crops, helped cattle to breed easily, and also protected against fire and lightning. Some of the log was also kept to rekindle the sacred fire again at the next Winter Solstice.

CHRISTMAS CANDLES

In some regions, notably Britain and Scandinavia, the Yule candle provided another sacred solar flame, and it was most important that it be kept burning for the required length of time, or dire consequences would ensue. Sometimes it had to be kept going for a whole day, sometimes it was relit every night from Christmas to New Year. As long as the flame flickered, it promised abundance in all things; to strengthen its beneficent powers, piles of money, clothing, food and drink were laid out within the circle of its golden rays. If the flame was allowed to die and darkness fell, it foreshadowed death.

To obtain full use of the candle's magic, its remains were not wasted but, like the ashes and remnants of the Yule log, used in various ways for good luck. In Sweden, for example, the plow was first smeared with leftover tallow before being used in Spring.

THE GHOST OF CHRISTMAS PAST

If we compare our Bacchanalian Christmases and New Year-tides with these Saturnalia and Feasts of Janus, we shall finde such affinitye between them ... that wee must needs conclude the one to be the very ape or issue of the other.
(HISTRIOMASTIX, WILLIAM PRYNNE, 1632)

The imitative magic of the midwinter fires was one way to call back the Sun, but it was not the only means available to deliver the infant of promise out of the darkness. Just as flame can cleanse and destroy, so the behavior of man can speed up the process of purification needed to bring the new out of the old. The seasonal excesses of Christmas and New Year—two faces of the same rite—have fundamentally this purpose.

Fröhliche Weihnachten!

At a superficial level, of course, the merrymaking of this time has a straightforward celebratory nature. At another level, however, it is an enactment of the death throes of the old rule, whose decline, like that of any living system, is marked by fragmentation, disintegration and decay. Going even deeper still, these Winter Solstice rites signify not just an annual death and beginning, but also the very Beginning, when the world was born from the womb of Chaos. Such symbolism was hugely important—if Creation could triumph over Destruction, if the God could vanquish Death and be reborn, then man, too, might survive—for another year, at least.

Various Winter Solstitial festivals and traditions express this death of the outgoing order as a descent into anarchy. The most famous of them is the Saturnalia of ancient Rome, originally celebrated on December 19. Then, when the calendar was changed by Julius Caesar, the festival moved to December 17, and was gradually extended until it finally lasted seven days, from December 17 to 23.

The Saturnalia commemorated a Golden Age once presided over by the Roman fertility god, Saturn. Like all good things, however, Saturn's reign had to come to an end. As the old monarch relinquished his throne and abandoned himself to oblivion, the world he ruled was turned topsy-turvy. In Rome all work ceased, including warring, criminals went unpunished, schools closed, language was free and unbridled, sexual inhibitions were thrown to the winds, gambling was rife, dress codes relaxed as simple tunics replaced the toga, and masters and mistresses waited on their slaves.

After only a brief respite, the population of Rome then surged through the gateway of time guarded by the god Janus, Keeper of the Portals of Heaven, to arrive in January, the month named after the god. As is wholly appropriate for this guardian of the door, Janus had two faces—one that could look back at the past and one forward into the future. On January 1, the Calends began. New consuls took office, and the celebrations lasted at least three days. Again a mood of anarchy prevailed, and many of the features of the

January Calends are echoed in modern Christmas and New Year customs. There were processions on the eve of the festival and few people bothered to go to bed, spending the night parading the streets, indulging in singing and all kinds of merrymaking. As dawn broke, they decorated their houses with laurels and other forms of greenery and then sank into bed to sleep it off, for many then—as now—felt it necessary to partake freely of the "flowing bowl."

Roman-style midwinter revelry was adopted by the followers of Christ. The Catholic Church was prepared to allow such pagan jollity, provided it was given a Christian gloss. Centuries later, however, the Puritans not only attacked what they called the "abuses" but also tried to ban Christmas itself by turning feast into fast, a strategy formerly used by Catholics. In England in 1644, fate played into the Puritans' hands when Christmas Day happened to fall on the last Wednesday of the month, ordained by Parliament as a regular fast day. On that day, as on every other Christmas Day through to 1656, Parliament sat, but the shopkeepers, in true seasonal spirit, kept their shops firmly shut—it was not to be business as usual. Across the Atlantic in Massachusetts, seventeenth-century American Puritans also tried to ban Christmas. Needless to say, neither group met with any success.

AN END AND A BEGINNING

I am Alpha and Omega, the beginning and
the ending …
(*REVELATION*, CHAPTER 1, VERSE 10)

Other peoples, at other times, had their own ways of honoring this momentous transition from old to new, at whatever date their New Year might fall. In ancient Babylon, for example, in the *Akîtu* celebrations, people staged not just seasonal rebirth out of death, but—for greatest effect—the very first birth of all, the Creation. First, the Creation story, the *Enûma elis*, was recited several times, after which two groups of actors would mime the victorious birth struggles of the god Marduk from the formless, watery womb of Tiamat, the Mother Goddess also known as the Deep (a birth that may also be seen as a triumph of a male god over a female).

SINS OF THE FLESH

Especially in Christmas tyme there is nothing els vsed but cardes, dice, tables, maskyng, mumming, bowling, and suche like fooleries; and the reason is, that they think they haue a commission and prerogatiue that tyme to doe what they list, and to followe what vanities they will. But (alas!) doe they thinke that they are preuiledged at that time to doe euill? The holier the time is (if one time were holier than an other, as it is not), the holier ought their exercises to bee. Can any tyme dispence with them, or giue them libertie to sinne? No, no; the soule which sinneth shall dye, at what tyme soeuer it offendeth…. Notwithstandyng, who knoweth not that more mischeef in that tyme committed than in all the yere besides?
(*ANATOMIE OF ABUSES*, PHILIP STUBBES, 1583)

During the ancient Egyptian turn of the year celebrations, magical rituals reminded the new God of his recurring victory over the old. Each year, in the eternal cycle, the red-haired god Set, to whom the ass was sacred, murdered his brother Osiris, the vegetation god of Egypt (and also bull god), and every New Year (which in ancient Egypt fell on July 20) Osiris was triumphantly conceived again as the Nile fooded. The Egyptians celebrated Set's defeat by rolling red-haired men in the mud, and even going so far as to drive asses over cliffs. Thus, in symbolic manner, the ass-god of the Old Year was driven out, and the way was cleared for the coming of the new Divine Child.

In parts of England and Ireland, the Old Year was seen out and the New Year welcomed in with the custom of "hunting the wren," usually on St. Stephen's Day, December 26, also known as Boxing Day (a similar custom was observed in ancient Greece and Rome). According to British folklore, the Robin is the Spirit of the New Year who sets out, birch rod in claw, to hunt his predecessor, the Gold Crest Wren, the Spirit of the Old Year, hiding in an ivy bush. With its blood-red chest, the Robin is said to have "murdered his father." The practice itself involved "wren boys" ceremonially hunting a real wren, and then decorating and parading its body in a religious procession. At all other times of year, the wren was protected, and it was considered very unlucky to steal its eggs. In Rome, both the Wren and its ivy were sacred to Saturn, the merry old king whose reign came to an end at the Winter Solstice.

In Scotland, where New Year has always been a more important festival than Christmas, the last day of the year is known as Hogmanay. A New Year custom that is particularly popular among Scots is that of the First Footer, also known as the Lucky Bird or Holly Boy. As the clock strikes midnight, people prepare for a visitation from this Spirit of the Season.

Since his nature will determine the household's fortunes for the coming year, certain characteristics are desirable and others are not. The first foot over the threshold should be that of a tall, well-made man, ideally of dark coloring— as suits the "saturnine" appearance of this messenger from Saturn, the king who is handing over his throne to his successor (red-haired men and women are considered most unlucky). He should not be a lawyer, doctor, clergyman, or policeman, nor should he wear black or carry any sharp-edged tool, such as a knife. What he must do is to come bearing gifts of a loaf of

OPPOSITE: The Babylonion conqueror god Marduk sets off on his mission of matricide—to cleave in two the body of his mother, Tiamat, the "Deep," and so divide the waters, as Jehovah later did when creating heaven and earth.

bread, a bottle of whisky, a lump of coal, and a silver coin, all magic charms ensuring an abundance of food, warmth and wealth. The ritual of his entry must be conducted in total silence, and no one may speak until the First Footer has given the coal to the fire, poured a glass for the head of the household, and blessed those assembled with "A happy New Year."

Another simple, but highly symbolic, ritual at the stroke of midnight is to open the back door to let the Ghost of the Old Year out, and open the front door to allow the Spirit of the New Year in.

THE FEAST OF FOOLS

Continuing the tradition of Saturnalian mayhem, the Feast of Fools was another entertainment enjoyed shortly after Christmas, particularly in France. Also known by the Latin name *Asinaria Festa*, or Feast of the Ass, it included a real ass in a starring role. This animal, supposedly, represented the beast on which Mary rode in the Flight into Egypt, or alternatively the one on which Christ made his triumphant entry into Jerusalem. The ass, however, also had a much older, pre-Christian connection with the Winter Solstice. Among its ancestors were the *cervulus*, or hobby-buck, of the Roman Calends, and Set, the ass-god, whose defeat was celebrated at the ancient Egyptian New Year.

Although there may have been local differences in the detail of the Feast, it seems that the ass was usually allowed inside the church to play its part. In one variation, it was led in procession into the building on January 1, the Feast of the Circumcision. The worshippers chanted the normal words of the service but, instead of saying "amen," brayed like asses. In another version, a girl with a baby in her arms rode the ass into the church on January 14; at the end of the service the priest brayed three times, with the congregation responding in a similar manner.

MERRY MONARCHS

Leading the solstice revelers in their celebrations was a merry monarch, elected to rule from Christmas to Twelfth Night (which was Christmas Day, Old Style). In Rome, this mock king was chosen by lot to preside over the Saturnalia festivities. His every command had to be obeyed, and, as one observer reported, he could tell a person to "shout out a libel on himself, another dance naked, or pick up the flute-girl and carry her thrice around the house." This figure may originally have been a stand-in for Saturn himself, and may, at the end of his reign, have been offered in ritual sacrifice in place of the god.

Later, notably in medieval and Tudor England and France, the mock king was known as the Lord of Misrule, who presided over the Feast of Misrule. He also went by the names of King or Abbot of Misrule and, in Scotland, Master or Abbot of Unreason, who might have at his disposal an "army" of twenty to sixty officers, musicians, dragons and hobby-horses.

On Twelfth Night, another king appeared—the King of the Bean, or Twelfth Night King, who ruled the celebrations for the day. He was chosen by means of a bean hidden in the special cake made for the occasion; whoever got the slice containing the bean became king. This monarch of medieval France and England was a descendant of the ceremonial king chosen at the Twelfth Night festival in ancient Rome. Known as the "Festival of Kings Created by Beans," this also involved "choice by bean." Beans were an ancient female fertility symbol that also had connotations of resurrection. To gain royal status, Roman men had to draw black or white beans, symbolizing women; dice later replaced the beans. In French and English tradition, the King acquired his Queen when a woman chose the slice of Twelfth Cake containing a pea.

Another seasonal "lord" was the medieval Boy Bishop, a choir-boy appointed to the position by other members of the choir on January 5, the Eve of Saint Nicholas. This "bishop" wore the clothes of his office and dispensed benediction, while his peers in the choir dressed as dean, archdeacon and canons. During his brief term of office, the Boy Bishop and his followers also had the right to be served supper by the Dean or one of his canons.

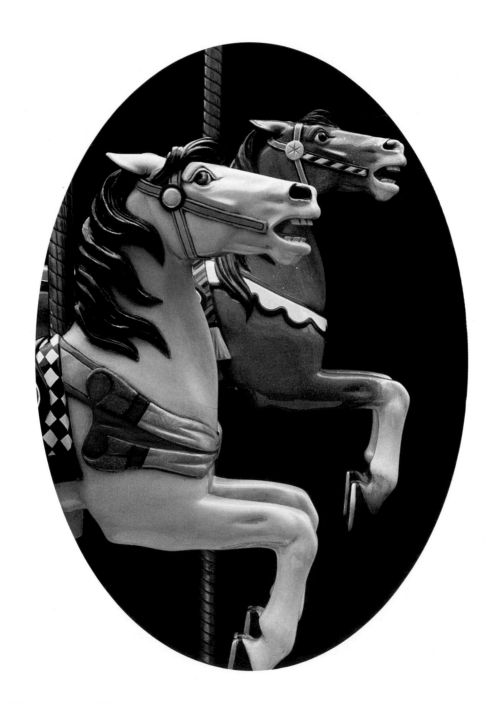

ENTER THE PLAYERS

Yet another host of anarchic figures could be seen during Yuletide in the boisterous entertainments and burlesques of the season. During this period as well as at other times of the year, sword dances were performed in various parts of Europe. In these, one observer remarked, "naked youths, who profess this sport, fling themselves in dance among swords and levelled lances." In some versions, the swords were brought down on a player's head, or placed in a circle around his neck, in a mock execution. Sometimes the sword dancers wore jingling bells, making them similar to the traditional English morris dancers. With less dancing and more drama, the English mummers' plays presented the eternal theme of death and revival; their usual storyline centered on a violent fight, followed by the arrival of a "doctor" who would bring the dead back to life.

Both kinds of dance had characters in common. "Tommy" of the sword dance and the Fool of the morris dance wore the skin and tail of a fox or other animal, while the sword dance's "Bessy" and the morris dance's "Maid Marian" were men dressed as women. These are clearly the descendants of figures from the Roman Calends, the Dionysian ceremonies, and beyond— the "animal-man" and his ancestor, the hunter for whom killing an animal was a sacred rite; and the "woman-man," representative of the real women who were once guardians of the rites of vegetation and the Earth. The hobby-horse also put in frequent appearances in both dances, while Saint George, or "Green George," the central figure of the mummers' plays, is really a spirit of Spring showing up early at Christmas.

In comes I, Old Father Christmas
Welcome or welcome not,
I hope Old Father Christmas
Will never be forgot.
If you don't believe what I do say
Enter St. George and clear the way.
In come I, St. George,
A man of courage bold
With sword and spear all by my side,
Hoping to gain a crown of gold.
'Twas I that slew the dragon,
and brought him to the slaughter,
And by those means I hope
To gain the King of Egypt's daughter.

(TRADITIONAL MUMMERS' PLAY)

MAKING A SONG AND DANCE

Another seasonal activity that involved dancing was carol-singing. Carols originally had no religious significance in the modern sense, but were a joyful way of celebrating the sacred mysteries through song and dance, which, for pagans, went naturally together. A carol was once a ring-dance accompanied by singing. In twelfth century France, the carols that greeted the coming of Spring were amorously playful song-dances. In Italy and in England, from

OPPOSITE: An archetypal symbol of wild Nature, the horse in various guises appeared in the Midwinter festivities. These fairground horses capture the essence of the animal's wildness.

the thirteenth to the sixteenth century, the term was similarly understood as a song accompanied by dancing.

Carol singing also involved processions, as revelers went from house to house carrying magical objects such as evergreen branches, to bestow a blessing on all they met. In parts of Europe, for example, it was the custom for a group of clergy and choir boys, dressed in pure white, and carrying a crucifix, to walk around the villages, singing songs of the Nativity, and receiving some money in return. Much earlier in time, however, this procession would have celebrated a different deity; instead of the crucifix, it would have carried a figure of the god Bel, also known as Marduk, the Great Lord of the Babylonians.

VISITORS FROM THE OTHERWORLD

Twas the night before Christmas,
when all through the house
Not a creature was stirring, not even a mouse;
The stockings were hung in the chimney with care,
In hopes that St. Nicholas soon would be there.
(THE NIGHT BEFORE CHRISTMAS,
CLEMENT C. MOORE, 1779-1863)

Carol-singers, Fools, and Merry Monarchs were not the only anarchic figures abroad at Yuletide. Whenever the normal laws of existence collapse, however briefly—as they do at the Winter Solstice and other important hinges in the wheel of time—supernatural beings take the opportunity to enter the world of man. At Yule, the most familiar visitor from the Otherworld is, of course, Santa Claus, that figure of mystery who comes secretly in the middle of the night and who has delighted, excited and tantalized generations of children who see him as the main point of Christmas.

Santa is said to have been based on Saint Nicholas, who in the Christian calendar has his feast day on December 6 (which may be a form of late "Halloween"), and on which children in continental Europe are traditionally given sweets, left overnight in their shoes. This saint, a fourth-century bishop

ABOVE: In this 1905 illustration by Arthur Rackham, a short, fat, jolly "Father Christmas" or Santa Claus confronts a thin, ragged Scrooge figure.

RIGHT: Wild dancers cavort around a composed young woman, perhaps representing the Virgin, in this medieval entertainment.

from Myra in Asia Minor, was the very model of propriety and Christian virtue. As a baby, he would only suckle from his mother's breast once on fast days, and later saved three young women from prostitution by throwing three golden balls for their dowries through their windows one night. His most celebrated miracle, however, was bringing back to life three murdered boys who had been pickled in a tub of brine. For this, Saint Nicholas was made the patron saint of children, "Santa Claus" being a corruption of his name via the Dutch "Sinte Klaas."

We are so familiar with the jolly Santa Claus figure that we don't even think to check his credentials before allowing him down the chimney—but stop and consider! Is night-riding with a horde of animal "familiars," arriving at midnight, expecting food offerings to be left out for him, and living in the darkness of the far North the kind of behavior one expects of a Christian saint? The truth is that Santa Claus is not the only seasonal bringer of gifts—he has a whole team of competitors and helpers of pre-Christian lineage, who appear at different times during the season from Saint Nicholas' Eve to Twelfth Night, and to whom the latter-day Santa is much more likely to be related than to the pious Nicholas.

Santa's prototype may not have been an old man but an old woman, who in Teutonic lore went by the names of Frau Berchte, Perchta, Holde, Holle or Buzebergt, or, in Italy, Befana or La Strega, "the Witch." Berchte and Befana were both connected with Twelfth Night, the eve of the Epiphany, or the arrival of the Magi at Christ's birthplace. The word epiphany may be a corruption of "Befana," and the day is also known in German as the *Berchtentag*, or Berchte's day. Call the old woman what you will, her hag-like appearance reveals her kinship with the Goddess in her third aspect as Dame Death, the Dark Moon that presides over Winter. Sometimes she was benign, sometimes punitive, depending on the behavior of mortals and which of her personalities she had adopted for the occasion.

In Scandinavia, Santa's cousin was the goblin-like, grandfather figure, Tomte Gubbe. He may have represented the ghost of the founder of the family and, as with all supernatural beings whose powers were greater than those of humans, his goodwill had to be earned. Accordingly, on Christmas Eve, a bowl of Yule porridge and fresh milk was left out for his visit, as well as a suit of small clothes as befitted his stature, some alcohol, and even some tobacco.

SANTA'S HELPERS

Santa's co-workers are a curiously unchristian-like crowd, and reveal that this jolly old uncle has a dark as well as a light face. In parts of Germany, Switzerland and Austria, Saint Nicholas traditionally came attired in the gorgeous robes of a bishop, and, to children who could recite their prayers, offered rewards of sweets; those who could not, however, he referred to his alter ego, an apparition known as the *Klaubauf*, who stood, rod in hand—a terrifying, shaggy, horned monster, with black face, red eyes, long red tongue and clanking chains, the personification of the Christian Devil.

The Klaubauf and other related beasts belong to the family of Teutonic Yuletide animals that includes the *Schimmelreiter* or the *Klapperbock*—a kind of hobby-horse with moving jaws that snaps at children who do not know their prayers—and the Mari Llwyd of the Welsh Christmas. This consisted of a real horse's skull, dressed up with ribbons, at the end of a pole disguised by a white cloth. A man underneath the cloth operated the jaws, and the phantom horse chased after everyone, biting its victims and only releasing them on payment of a fine. The "Old Hob" of England appeared throughout the Winter period, and similar creatures were to be seen in Denmark, Sweden and Norway at Christmas. Such fake horses are imitations of the real ones that, in ancient Europe, were holy, sacrificial animals which would have been taken round in procession, like their hobby-horse descendants.

Animals featured strongly at the Roman Calends, too, when people wore animal masks, or even skins—a relic of the masquerades of the Dionysian festival which the Calends had replaced. Dressing up as an animal, or "beast-masking," derives from the most ancient magic. It was a way of uniting oneself with the magical and divine spirit of Nature, manifested in the Horned God, and in sacred animals.

Santa's night-riding follows shamanic tradition. Siberian and Lapp shamans used hallucinogens such as fly agaric, the "magic mushroom" to aid them in their "flight."

RIDERS ON THE STORM

The circumstances surrounding Santa's arrival give further clues to the man behind the mask. Coming down onto a rooftop with a team of twelve reindeer—and amid the jangle of elfin bells—cannot be a noiseless affair, as pointed out in Clement Moore's Victorian poem *The Night Before Christmas*, when "there arose such a clatter" as "Saint Nick" landed. The clamor of the horde is suggestive of *das wüthende Heer* (the raging host of riders) of the Christmas of German lore, and the "Yule host" of Iceland. In parts of England, the host took animal form and was known as the "Yeth (heathen) hounds" or "Wish hounds." In connection with the celestial train of dogs, Santa's familiar rivals, the Frauen, appear again. Frau Gaude and Frau Harke, sisters of Berchte, Perchta, Holde, et al, each has her pack of howling hounds, with whom she goes raging through the air at night.

Frau Gaude was also known as Frau Wode, from the old German word for fury. Wode has been connected with Woden, or Odin, the chief male deity of all the Teutonic peoples, the God of the Storm who led *das wüthende Heer* through the night sky. Woden decided man's destiny, and ruled with that most powerful of weapons—magic—determining the outcome of battles not with the sword, but with an enchantment: his *herfjöturr*, or "army fetter," was a spell that bewitched warriors into a paralyzing panic. He was the magician-god of the Otherworld; Yggdrasil—his sacred ash tree which supported the world, and which was also the "terrible horse" or "horse of Ygg (Ogre)" may, at least once, have been his battle steed, conjuring a spine-tingling picture of this Shaman of the Universe riding the crest of the storm like some wild witch on a broomstick.

"Flying" is an activity that Santa shares not only with the divine Woden but also with the real, flesh-and-blood shamans—magician-priests—of Siberia and Lapland, who used psychedelic substances such as fly agaric, or *Agaricus muscarius*, the "magic mushroom," to transport them into "flight." Like these inhabitants of the frozen North, Santa lives as far north as it is possible to go, way beyond the cozy Christian realm of St. Nicholas. For 364 days of the year, he dwells in polar darkness, in the place where the Norns, the Three Fates of Norse legend (the original owners of Yggdrasil) turn the Millwheel of the

NIGHT FLIGHT

Woden, the Frauen, and Santa were not the only ones who might indulge in night-riding over Christmas. In Scotland, on December 12, St. Finnian's Night, it was very important to eat well before retiring. Those who went to bed without supper risked being carried over the rooftop by supernatural beings, as in the following incident reported by an English clergyman in 1683:

Francis Fry returning from Work was caught by the Woman Specter by the Skirts of his Doublet, and carried into the Air … and about half an Hour after he was heard Whistling and Singing in a Kind of a Quagmire. Coming to himself an Hour after, he solemnly protested, that the Daemon carried him so high he saw his Master's House underneath him no bigger than an Hay-cock … he prayed God not to suffer the Devil to destroy him; and he was then suddenly set down in that Quagmire. The workmen found one Shoe on one side of the House, and the other shoe on the other side; his Perriwig was espied next Morning hanging on top of a Tall Tree.

Universe. Here, too, is where the great Celtic dead go when they die, to the castle "at the back of the North Wind."

A FATEFUL TIME

As the Old Year relaxes its hold and supernatural forces break free, so the whole period of the Twelve Days lasting into the New Year, as well as the few days before Christmas, is a time for looking into the future.

The fact that there are twelve days is significant. The Babylonians used this number in their *Akîtu* ceremonies, which also went on for twelve days and celebrated their New Year. Part of the *Akîtu* was a "Festival of the Fates," known as *Zagmuk*, a ritual which involved looking at the omens for each of the twelve months to come. As a mini-model of the year, the *Zagmuk* effectively "magicked" it into being. (This was the Egyptian twelve-month year, rather than the druidic thirteen-month year).

Another profoundly fateful influence at this time is that of the ever-present Frauen, Santa's cousins. As they do their rounds during the Twelve Nights, they dispense good or bad fortune in the form of rewards and punishments. They are said to allow no spinning during their visiting time, and to punish girls who have unspun flax still on their distaffs. The Frauen are the "spinster" goddesses of spinning—and spinning is, of course, the task of the Fates, who weave the fortunes of mankind with the yarn of destiny. In an English Christmas tradition, the Frauen are replaced by the Devil, Lord of Hell—but he may have stolen his persona from one of them, Frau Holde, who is also Mother Holle or Hel, Queen of the Underworld, and from whom we get our word "Hell."

BEARER OF FATE

Santa Claus' kinship to the world magician Woden and the fate-bearing Frauen is appropriate: as gift-bringer, this spirit of Christmas is also a Master of Fate, for "Christmas presents" were once given to ensure good luck.

A feature of the Roman midwinter festivities, for example, was the giving of gifts known as *strenae* because they consisted simply of branches plucked

ABOVE: Each of the decorations on the evergreen Christmas tree, and each of the gifts below it, is essentially a wish, a magic charm to bring good fortune.

OVERLEAF: Winter solstice sunrise at Swinside stone circle in Yorkshire.

in the sacred grove of the goddess Strenia. Taken from the trees that embodied the vegetation spirit, these early *strenae* were fertility charms to ensure fruitfulness in the year to come. The imitation fruits later exchanged at the Saturnalia had the same magical purpose.

Another kind of present the Romans gave were little figures made of clay or paste. The traditional German biscuit figures hung on the Christmas tree may be a lingering vestige of these dolls, which symbolized earlier human sacrificial victims, and were again offerings for good fortune.

As well as charms to encourage general fertility, Roman presents could also achieve other effects, such as prosperity or well-being. Thus people gave "honeyed things, that the year of the recipient might be full of sweetness, lamps that it might be full of light, copper and silver and gold that wealth might flow in amain." (*The Mediaeval Stage*, E. K. Chambers, 1903)

THE WEIRD SISTERS

Modranicht—meaning the night of mothers—was the name given by the Venerable Bede (c.673-735), the English theologian, to Christmas Eve, a night when gifts of food might be left out for beings from the spirit world, just as we now leave Santa Claus something to eat and drink. Christians would offer food to their own mother figure, the Virgin Mary, but even as late as the eleventh century, others expected visitations from women whom they called the Three Sisters. Known throughout the ancient world by a myriad of names, such as the Parcae in ancient Rome, or the Norns in Northern Europe, these beings were, in fact, none other than the Three Fates, those Weird Sisters who spun the threads of wyrd—man's destiny—or who, as fairies, came to bless or curse a newborn child.

PREDICTING THE FUTURE

There were many Yuletide practices that offered a glimpse into the future, especially in those vital concerns, love and marriage. Here are just a few:

• To ascertain her future husband's trade, a girl should pour melted lead into cold water and watch the shapes it forms. If she sees a plane, a last, or a pair of scissors, her husband will be a carpenter, shoemaker, or tailor; if she sees a hammer or pickax, he will be a smith or a laborer.

• To find out who will marry first, a group of girls should blindfold a gander and then stand in a circle, with the gander in their midst. Whoever he goes to first will be the first bride.

• Anyone who wishes to know the future should put their ear to the baking-oven. If music is heard, there will be a wedding soon, but if bells ring out, the listener will die.

TALKING ANIMALS

Although animals are said to acquire the gift of speech around Christmastime, it is not wise to try to listen in on their conversation. One man, who was foolish enough to doubt that animals could talk, hid himself in his master's stable on Christmas Eve. At the stroke of midnight, the beasts began a conversation:

"We shall have hard work to do in a week's time," said one of the great horses that stood in the stable.

"Yes," replied the other, "for the farmer's servant is heavy."

"And the road to the graveyard is steep and long …" added the first.

A week later, the two horses pulled the listener's coffin to its burying ground.

WATER INTO WINE

One of the more fortunate effects of the supernatural current with which Christmastime is charged is that water commonly turns to wine on Christmas Eve. As always, however, one should never question any boons from the Otherworld. One Frenchwoman who did went to the well at midnight to check the water-into-wine theory. As she drew up her bucket, she heard a voice echoing from the depths of the well, saying:

"Toute l'eau se tourne en vin,
Et tu es proche de ta fin." (All the water is turned into wine, and you are approaching your end.) Soon after, the woman was afflicted with a fatal disease, and died within the year.

NEW WATER

Water is a highly charged substance, being the current that carries life, but at such an auspicious time as New Year, it becomes even more magically potent. In Britain and other parts of Europe, there was a belief in the power of "new water," the first water of the year to be drawn from the well. In one tradition, as the clock struck midnight, people rushed with their pitchers to be the first to collect the "cream of the well," and the good fortune that went with it. In another, someone went in silence to the well to draw a pitcherful of water on New Year's Eve. This magic draft would be taken on New Year's morning.

GIFT ORDER

During the New Year festivities in ancient Rome, it was the custom for both senators and the people to offer up wishes—*vota*—for the prosperity of the Emperor in the coming year. They were also expected to give him *strenae* in the form of money. In a display of unabashed greed which caused much public resentment, the Emperor Caligula not only issued an order making these *strenae* compulsory but also stood in the entrance to his palace to receive them in person.

MAGICAL CHARMS

As late as the fifteenth century, present-giving still retained its old magical purpose, as described in this list of complaints by a Bohemian monk, who erroneously believed that the custom originally had a Christian intention:

• Instead of giving presents in memory of "God's great Gift to man," the monk said, they were given for good luck, because anyone who did not give freely would be unlucky in the coming year.

• Instead of giving money to the poor, people laid it on the table as a charm to bring wealth. Purses were also left open to allow good luck to enter.

• Instead of using fruit to symbolize "Christ the Precious Fruit," it was cut open and used to tell fortunes. (The fruit may well have been the apple, the Goddess's sacred fruit; when cut open, the pips of the apple form the magic pentagram.)

• Instead of making large white loaves as symbols of the "True Bread," they were left out so that the gods might eat them.

CHAPTER 5

A MIDNIGHT FEAST

DECEMBER 21: WINTER SOLSTICE;
CHRISTMAS AND NEW YEAR

At Christmas be merry and thankful withall
And feast thy poor neighbours, the great
with the small.
Yea, all the year long, to the poor let us give
God's blessing to follow us while we do live.

(FIVE HUNDRED POINTS OF GOOD HUSBANDRY,

THOMAS TUSSER, 16TH CENTURY)

D eep in the bleak midwinter mankind celebrates the return of the solar and savior god with the grandest birthday party of the entire year, to which all are invited. Preparations may begin weeks, or even months, ahead, as seasonal dishes are made ready for the great day. In some countries the sacred feast begins on the eve of December 25, the old date of the Winter Solstice; in others, it is held on the day itself.

To increase the air of optimism, homes are decorated with traditional greenery—holly, mistletoe, and, of course, the Christmas tree, dazzling with lights, glitter, and jeweled baubles like some fairy tree from an Aladdin's cave. These evergreens, undying in the midst of winter when most other plants are bare, are tokens of promise that life will renew itself once more.

DECEMBER

THE SACRED FEAST

Everywhere we find that a sacrifice ordinarily involves a feast, and that a feast cannot be provided without a sacrifice. For a feast is not complete without flesh, and in early times the rule that all slaughter is sacrifice was not confined to the Semites. The identity of religious occasions and festal seasons may indeed be taken as the determining characteristic of the type of ancient religion generally; when men meet their god they feast and are glad together, and whenever they feast and are glad they desire that the god should be of the party.
(LECTURES ON THE RELIGION OF THE SEMITES,
W. ROBERTSON SMITH, 1894)

The orgy of eating and drinking over Christmas is an echo of a pagan feast, but without its sacrificial element. Like the giving of presents, Christmas fare may originally have been intended as a charm, based on the magical principle that like produces like—if food and drink were plentiful at this most auspicious time of year, they would be plentiful throughout the coming year, too.

Christmas dishes vary from country to country, but there are two in particular which are very interesting for their magical symbolism. One is the Yule log—once fuel for a real sacred fire but now found mainly as a cylindrical cake, coated in chocolate marked to represent bark. The other is traditional roast sucking pig, served with an apple in its mouth. The pig was sacred to the Goddess in her death aspect—the Sow—goddess, known as Cerridwen to the Celts, Freya to the Scandinavians,

Christmas falls at the end of Capricorn, the sign of the Horned Goat. Here, a figure astride a goat toasts all from a steaming bowl.

Astarte to the Assyrians, Demeter to the Greeks. Throughout the Indo-European world there were boar-gods, representing the Goddess's murdered lover and son-to-be. In Athens, Demeter accepted his death in the annual pig sacrifice enacted in midwinter; pigs were also sacrificed to Astarte, whose sacred Winter Solstice mysteries in Syria and Egypt celebrated the birth of the new solar god. In India the boar-god was Vishnu, and in Scandinavia he was Heimdall.

At Yule, Heimdall was sacrificed with an apple in his mouth. Of all fruits, the apple was the most sacred. It was the very container of life itself, the Goddess's magic fruit of immortality, which she kept in her paradise garden in the west. In Norse mythology, the goddess Idun allowed the gods to eat of her apple so that they would have eternal life. The apple contained the essence of being– the soul—which could be passed from one body to another by eating the fruit. Thus the apple in the boar-god's mouth was his soul that would give the God life again.

In Denmark and Sweden, another tradition that preserves the God's soul at Yule is to bake a pig-shaped loaf, known as the Yule Boar. The flour used to make the loaf comes from the last sheaf of corn to be harvested. The Yule Boar is kept on the table throughout the Christmas period, and is sometimes even saved until Spring, when part is mixed with the new seed, and part given to the plowman and his animals to eat. In this way, the continuation of the God's life cycle is ensured. The spirit of the Corn King, cut down in his prime at harvest-time, is held in the loaf so that he may rise again at Yule as the boar-god, and in Spring as the new Lord of Fertility who gives life to the crops.

As was the custom further south, a real boar was

once sacrificed in Scandinavia, as was a human representative of the boar-god. In Sweden, a Yule custom lingered in which a man, wrapped in a skin and with wisps of straw "bristles" sticking out of his mouth, was symbolically murdered by that familiar figure, an old woman, with blackened face, wielding a knife.

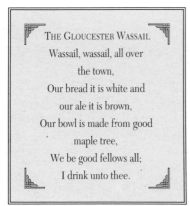

Laden with snow and sparkling with lights, a Christmas tree "comes alive" in the forest.

YOUR GOOD HEALTH

The warming punch that is so welcome during the chill nights of Christmas is reminiscent of the old English wassail, a drink of hot, spiced ale and apples, also known as lamb's wool. The name wassail derives from the Anglo-Saxon toast *wes hál*, or "be whole": wassailing essentially meant drinking to someone's good health, and was a communal activity. Bearing the large wassail bowl, carol singers went from house to house, and at each the container from which everyone drank was topped up with the potent brew. The origins of the custom are not clear, but drinking the blood-dark draught may have begun as a means of communing with the divine that was later extended into a rite for the welfare of others.

A further extension was to bless the fruit trees, and so induce them to produce good crops the following year. This was known as "wassailing the orchards" and was done on Christmas Eve, New Year, or Twelfth Night. A party of people, including the farmer and his servants, would carry a large jug of alcoholic cider to the orchard, where they would encircle the largest tree and toast its health three times with a special incantation. They would then splash or sprinkle the tree with the cider. Alternatively, the tree would be hung with cider-soaked cakes, sprinkled with cider and toasted as before. Sometimes these ceremonies of enchantment would even be led by the vicar of the parish!

THE TREE OF LIFE

In jolly hymns they praise the god of wine,
Whose earthen images adorn the pine,
And these are hung on high in honor of the vine.
("SATURNALIA TREE" IN THE *GEORGICS*,
VIRGIL, 70-19 B.C.)

The tree with the closest association with Christmas is, of course, the Christmas tree, and the practice of bringing a celebratory tree indoors at festival time was observed by our pagan forebears. In ancient Rome, on the night before a holy day, such as during the Saturnalia, priests known as *dendrophori* or "tree bearers" would go to the pinea silva, the sacred pine grove of the Goddess. There they would choose a pine, which they would ceremonially cut down, decorate, and bear back to the Goddess's temple to receive the effigy of the sacrificial god. Like the strenae, the branches from the grove that were the original Saturnalian gifts, this Roman pine with its pyramid form represented the fertilizing powers of the God, as does the modern *Weihnachtsbaum* or Christmas tree.

Understood another way, the tree also embodies the God himself as spirit of vegetation—and this tree is not only green but evergreen. Living when all else is dead, the Christmas tree promises rebirth, and a prayer for new life is at the heart of the midwinter festival.

The star at the top of the tree is a sign of hope, the Goddess rising as the Star of the Sea—call her Isis, Ishtar, Aphrodite, or Mary—to announce the birth of her own particular God. The figurines hanging from the branches are suggestive of once-real sacrificial victims and the savior God they represented, the vegetation spirit embodied in the tree who died and was reborn. The balls, baubles and bells are the burgeoning flowers and fruit of this reborn spirit of life, while the tree lights (formerly candles) are reminders of another life-force, the returning Sun.

Before the familiar conifer was adopted as a Christmas emblem, it was the custom to place boughs of fruiting trees such as cherry or hazel into pots or containers of water indoors, so that they would flower at Christmas or New Year. Continuing the fertility theme, there was also a popular belief that on

> ### EVERLASTING LIFE
> At their winter solstice festival, the Egyptians also decorated their homes with the Tree of Life, in their case with the date palm, which in ancient Egypt was the tree of immortality.

In Brough in the north-west of England, it was the custom to carry a flaming "holly tree" (a large branch) through the town on Twelfth Night. The parade was attended by a marching band, fireworks, and cheering crowds.

Christmas Eve, apple and other orchard trees blossomed and bore fruit. A Christian gloss was given to this in the famous legend of Saint Joseph of Arimathea. Joseph was a wealthy Jew from the Holy Land and a secret Christian, who lived in the first century A.D. He traveled to England and, on arriving at Glastonbury, planted his staff (a phallus-like rod) into the "earth" (the womb of the Great Mother) whereupon it immediately put forth leaves. This curious plant was known as the Glastonbury Thorn, and was said to blossom every Christmas Eve (Old Style).

In Alsace, now in eastern France, another tree ritual, similar to rites at other times of year (such as the dance around the May-pole at Beltane), again emphasizes fertility magic. On New Year's Eve, it was the custom for local girls to set up a small fir tree or holly bush, decorated with egg shells, ribbons, and small figures, above the village fountain. On the evening of the following day, they would dance and sing around the fountain, only allowing the boys to join them on request. The tree would be kept all year to protect those who had set it up.

THE HOLLY AND THE IVY

The holly and the ivy,
When they are both full grown,
Of all the trees that are in the wood,
The holly bears the crown:
The rising of the sun
And the running of the deer,
The playing of the merry organ,
Sweet singing in the choir.
(TRADITIONAL CAROL)

In the medieval Christmas carol "The Holly and the Ivy," with its powerful pagan flavor, we celebrate two plants that symbolize the rite of passage from death to rebirth. Holly was sacred to Mother Holle, the Goddess as Queen of the Underworld, or "Hel" (that same Frau Holde who did her rounds during the Twelve Nights). Holly was the preferred choice for magic wands among German witches who worshipped Holle.

With its spiraling growth habit, the ivy—like the vine and the bean—implied resurrection, and was the sacred plant of the reincarnated God under his names of Dionysus in ancient Greece and Osiris in ancient Egypt. In the cult of Dionysus, boughs of holly and ivy were arrayed around the doorways at his winter festival.

Perhaps in one of those patriarchal coups to which the Goddess was subject, Saturn—the Ghost of the Old Year and King of the Saturnalia—adopted both the ivy and the holly as his own. His club was made of holly, and the nest of his sacred bird, the Gold Crest Wren, was formed from ivy. As well as being used at the Roman Saturnalia, holly was also the emblem of the ass god. In the folk customs of Europe, particularly France, he appeared at the midwinter festival, at the end of which this god, later known as the "Christmas Fool," was killed by his rival. In these examples, both the holly and the ivy are connected with the Old Year, and are linked with the midwinter customs of Hunting the Wren and The Feast of Fools.

In the traditional Yule game involving "holly boys" and "ivy girls" in a contest of forfeits, holly represents the male players and ivy the female. Here, the rivalry between the pair is not, as one might think, between an Old and New Year, but derives from the harvest custom in which the final sheaf to be cut was bound with ivy, and presented as a kind of booby prize to the farmer who was last to bring in his harvest. This sheaf was known as the "Ivy Girl" and conferred bad luck on the recipient until the following harvest. The "Holly Boy" was Saturn's representative, and featured in the New Year custom of the "first footer" in which a dark man had to be the first to cross the threshold at the start of the year—a moment when women were elaborately kept out of the way. Thus in the Yule game, in rather misogynist fashion, the ill-omened Ivy Girl and the woman-shy Holly Boy became rivals in a battle of the sexes.

THE GOLDEN BOUGH

Some women have worn mistletoe about their necks or arms, thinking it will help them to conceive.
(*ADAM IN EDEN*, WILLIAM COLES, 1657)

The mistletoe now associated with Christmas (and in druidic and Norse tradition also with Midsummer) is one of the most magical and sexually potent of all plants. To Greek pagans, it was the famous Golden Bough (so-called because as its berries age, they take on the color of gold, the superlative metal). It was with this precious bough, plucked from an oak at the gate to the Underworld, that Aenaes was able to make his way safely through the dark regions to speak with his dead father.

The evergreen mistletoe thus had strong associations with fertility, and was present to bless the midwinter celebrations with its life-giving power. The practice of kissing under the mistletoe at Christmas derives from the cult of the oak god and his orgiastic fertility rites—of which the modern custom is a very pale imitation.

Taliesin, bard, magician and Merlin figure, was said to be the son of Cerridwen, the Celtic White Goddess, keeper of the Cauldron of Inspiration (and, under another name, of Regeneration). The main incident of the romance of Taliesin occurred at the Winter Solstice. It tells how the magician contrived to beat the twenty-four racehorses of King Maelgwn by means of twenty-four charred twigs of holly—as the winning rider passed each horse, he dispatched it by striking it with one of Taliesin's twigs. Thus, by means of his magic powers, Taliesin destroys the last twenty-four hours of the old Holly King's year, and allows the Divine Child, the new solar infant, to emerge triumphant.

UNDER THE KISSING BOUGH

- Whoever stands under the mistletoe may be given as many kisses as wished.
- With each kiss, a boy should pluck one of the berries from the mistletoe; when all the berries are gone, the kissing stops.
- If a man-servant refuses to bring ivy to a maid-servant to decorate the house, the maid has the right to refuse him kisses under the mistletoe.
- The mistletoe should be burned on Twelfth Night, or some of the young women and men who have kissed under it may never marry.

MISTLETOE THE HEALER

The Druids called mistletoe "all-heal" and it was said to have many properties, as well as being a fertility aid:

- A potion made of its berries given to a woman, a man, or an animal will make them fruitful.
- If a farmer gives a bunch of Christmas mistletoe to the first cow that calves in the New Year, it will bring health to the whole herd.
- Mistletoe cures various illnesses and complaints. As well as curing sterility, it controls epilepsy and other nervous disorders, treats poisoning, and is excellent for childhood diseases.
- "Mysceltowe layd to the head draweth out the corrupt humors."
- "All locks are opened by the herb Missell toe."

(In other words, the mystical "key" of the phallic mistletoe opens the "womb" of the chamber or Underworld, as in the legend of Aeneas.)

CHAPTER 4

THE MAIDEN
FEBRUARY 1: IMBOLC

This is the day of Bride
The Queen will come from the Mound;
This is the day of Bride
The serpent will come from the hole.

(TRADITIONAL RHYME)

The weeks that follow the festivities around the Winter Solstice can seem dreary in contrast, dragging on interminably and bringing with them rain, sleet, snow, gloom and darkness. Even though the days are gradually becoming longer, the sun does not yet have much strength and, in some climates, the months of January and February often bring the worst weather of the year. This is just when the promise of Spring is needed to revive the flagging spirits of mankind—and when Nature obligingly provides that promise with the first signs of new life. The first day of February is the old Celtic festival marking the reawakening of the earth, known as Imbolc, or Oimelc, a name derived from the Gaelic for ewe's milk after the lactating sheep that are feeding the first lambs of the new season at this time of year.

Imbolc does not bring with it a dramatic change from the apparent death of winter—the trees do not burst into blossom overnight, leaves do not immediately sprout from the branches, plants and flowers do not instantly carpet the earth. Growth is gradual and not necessarily apparent—seeds may lie hidden in the earth, slowly pushing the first shoots up through the soil, and yet to the observer above all may appear lifeless.

At Imbolc, the signs of new life may be almost imperceptible, but they are there if only one will take the trouble to look. Catkins bud on the bare branches, and snowdrops announce the stirring of spring; in their honor, Imbolc is also known as the Snowdrop Festival.

Above all, Imbolc is a celebration of newness—the promise of fertility, new life, and new hope. It falls in Aquarius, a sign associated with air, the east, and spring, and depicted as the Water Bearer carrying the Water of Life. Aquarius is also linked with the Star in the Tarot pack, a card that symbolizes hope.

The white of the Imbolc snowdrop is a color with similar associations of newness, and is also the color of the Goddess as Virgin, the New Moon—appropriately enough, for in the pagan calendar Imbolc is the festival that celebrates the transformation of the Goddess from the dark Crone of Winter to the radiant Virgin of Spring, bringing with her the promise of fertility to come.

THE RETURN OF THE MAIDEN

Long, long ago, so the ancient Greek story goes, mortals lived in endless summer, but a conflict among the gods brought winter to the world for the first time.

Demeter, goddess of the fertile land, had a daughter named Kore. One day, Kore was out in the meadows gathering flowers with her companions, when she noticed a narcissus of particular beauty, and stooped to pick it. As she did so, the ground burst open and out thundered Hades, Lord of the Underworld, in his chariot. He seized Kore and carried her away with him to his dark kingdom below the Earth.

When Demeter heard of the disappearance of her daughter, it was as if all light and life had gone out of the world. Flinging over her shoulder the somber veil of sorrow, the goddess flew like a bird over land and sea, seeking for her lost child. When at last she discovered the name of the thief—and that the Father God Zeus himself had conspired in the crime—she was beyond herself with rage and despair. She disguised herself as an old woman, and desolately wandered the world of man.

At last she came to the city of Eleusis, that was ruled by the wise king Celeus. No one there knew her true identity, and in the king's palace she became nurse to his infant son. One day, as she was about to give the child the gift of immortality by lowering him into the fire, his mother spied her, and Demeter was forced to reveal her true identity. With all the power of her divine majesty, she commanded that a temple be built for her in Eleusis, where the people might come to celebrate her mysteries. In gratitude to Celeus' family for their hospitality, she also imparted to their oldest son, Triptolemus, her secrets. She gave to him the first grain of corn, and taught him how to sow it that it might bring forth rich harvests. She showed him how to harness oxen to the plow, and gave him a winged chariot drawn by dragons that he might travel the world spreading his knowledge among all men.

But all that was yet to come, for first the goddess would have her revenge for the theft of her daughter. Seated in her temple at Eleusis, she vowed that the Earth would not bear any fruit until her daughter was returned to her. And so it was. For the first time, the corn would not grow, the fruit would not ripen, and Darkness, Famine, and Death spread a black cloak over the land. Every creature, every mortal was afflicted with a terrible and biting hunger.

In desperation, Zeus sent the rainbow-goddess Iris to plead with Demeter. Descending to Earth on her iridescent bridge, Iris begged Demeter to relent, but it was of no use. One by one, the gods came to plead, but still the land lay barren. At last, the only solution was for Zeus to command Hades to return Kore to her mother. Hades agreed—but Hades had already prepared himself for this moment.

While she was in his kingdom, Hades had offered Kore a pomegranate, the "apple with many seeds." Only four of the seeds had passed the unsuspecting girl's lips, but these had sealed her fate, for the magical pomegranate is the fruit of sexual union. Kore was now the wife of Hades, and had a new name: Persephone, Queen of the Underworld.

So Hades consented to release his wife—but only for part of the year. As his queen, he demanded, she must spend four months of each year in the dark realm with him—one month for every seed swallowed.

And so it was and so it is that when the Maiden departs, winter cloaks the world. And so it was and so it is that when the Maiden returns, the Earth blossoms with joy and Spring dances over the land.

(Although this famous story comes from classical Greece, when male gods had wrested from the Goddess much of her old power, it has a predominantly female cast. Kore, Demeter, and Persephone reflect the Goddess's three lunar faces of Maiden, Mother, and Crone; the returning Virgin also represents the spirit of vegetation.)

Hades, Lord of the Underworld, carries off Kore, daughter of Demeter, and makes her his bride. Her enforced stay in the infernal regions brings winter to the world above.

OUR LADY

At the time of Imbolc, the Virgin Goddess reveals herself in various personifications. The first is that of Mary, the Holy Virgin of the Catholic Church. In the Christian calendar, the day after Imbolc, February 2, is designated the Feast of the Purification, when the mother of Jesus went to the temple to be ritually cleansed after giving birth. According to Hebrew tradition, all new mothers had to be "purified" a certain number of days after childbirth—forty days if the child was a boy, eighty days for a girl. When Mary attended the temple and presented her new baby, she met the aged Simeon who prophesied that the infant would become "a light unto the Gentiles"—in other words, the Light of the World. In memory of this prophesy, candles are blessed in church on this day, and candlelit services are held, giving rise to the feast's other name, Candlemas.

It is significant that Mary becomes a virgin "again" and ready for pregnancy in spring at precisely the time that the Earth renews herself and prepares for her fruitfulness to come. Purification rituals are intended to banish the old in order to make way for the new, which is what both Earth and Mary are doing at this time. As always, the dating of important Christian feasts provides fascinating clues to the older festivals which they superseded.

The Goddess renews herself: Aphrodite, born from the wave of the sea, floats shoreward in her shell. This famous painting by Sandro Botticelli, dating from c.1482, is known as The Birth of Venus (Venus *was the Roman name for the Greek Aprhodite).*

SISTER BRIGIT

Another sacred Christian female figure, St. Brigit or Bride, also has her holy day on February 1. According to Christian tradition, she helped the Virgin Mary give birth to Jesus, hence her status as protectress of pregnant women and midwives. This Brigit was also said to be a nun who had founded a convent at Kildare in Ireland. Because she was said to have cared for Mary's cows, she was also known as Christ's Milkmaid.

On closer scrutiny, St. Brigit turns out, like the Virgin Mary, not to be solely a Christian figure. One hint of her other identity may be found in her nickname, Christ's Milkmaid, which brings to mind the lactating ewes of the Celtic Oimelc. The saint has other curious attributes, too. At her convent at Kildare, for example, the milk of her cows never ran dry—in fact, such was the generosity of their yield that their milk flooded out across the land to form Loch Lemnacht, the Lake of New Milk. Spring was also said to blossom continually in the Saint's bower, and flowers and shamrocks sprang up wherever she placed her foot.

This lady, of course, was not only a saint, but originally a Celtic goddess, adopted and adapted to a Christian role. One of the most ancient and important Celtic deities, Brigit was the triple goddess of the empire of Brigantia which stretched across parts of Spain, France, and Britain. In her divine trinity, she governed fertility and healing, knowledge—the female arts of leechcraft, agriculture and inspiration—and smithcraft or firecraft. Her three personae were called the Three Mothers or the Three Blessed Ladies of Britain, and were associated with the Moon.

One of Brigit's earliest shrines was at Brigeto in Illyria, the old name for the northwestern part of the Balkan peninsula. Traveling northwards with Gaelic Celts, she finally arrived in Ireland. She had an exclusively female priesthood and men may have been barred from her cult, as suggested by her

The Virgin Mary was "remade" at the Feast of the Purification—cleansed of the act of giving birth.

As the sole remnant in Christianity of the female principle in the divine, from the Dark Ages onwards the Virgin Mary was slowly invested with all the attributes once shared between the many personifications of the Goddess, including Queen of Heaven. Just as Roman Catholics are encouraged to pray to Our Lady so that she may mediate, on their behalf, with God, so, in Apuleius' *The Golden Ass*, written in the second century A.D., the character Lucius begs the aid of another, pagan Queen of Heaven:

"O blessed Queen of Heaven … thou, which doth illuminate all the cities of the earth by thy feminine light; thou, which nourishest all the seeds of the world by thy damp heat … by whatsoever name or fashion or shape it is lawful to call upon thee, I pray thee to end my great travail and misery …"

In answer to his prayer, the Goddess reveals herself in all her universal and age-old glory. Rising Moon-like above the sea, she addresses him with the following words:

"Behold, Lucius, I am come; thy weeping and prayer hath moved me to succor thee. I am she that is the natural mother of all things, mistress and governess of all the elements, the initial progeny of worlds, chief of the powers divine, queen of all that are in Hell, the principal of them that dwell in Heaven, manifested alone and under one form of all the gods and goddesses. At my will the planets of the sky, the wholesome winds of the seas, and the lamentable silences of hell be disposed; my name, my divinity is adored throughout the world, in divers manners, in variable customs, and by many names. For the Phrygians that are the first of all men call me the Mother of the Gods at Pessinus; the Athenians, which are sprung from their own soil, Cecropian Minerva; the Cyprians, which are girt about by the sea, Paphian Venus; the Cretans which bear arrows, Dictynnian Diana; the Sicilians, which speak three tongues, Infernal Prosperpine; the Eleusinians, their ancient goddess Ceres; some Juno, other Bellona, other Hecate, other Rhamnusia, and principally both sort of the Ethiopians which dwell in the Orient and are enlightened by the morning rays of the sun, and the Egyptians, which are excellent in all kind of ancient doctrine and by their proper ceremonies accustomed to worship me, do call me by true name, Queen Isis. Behold, I am come to take pity of thy fortune and turbulation; behold I am present to favor and aid thee; leave off thy weeping and lamentation, put away all thy sorrow, for behold the healthful day which is ordained by my providence."

(TRANSLATED BY WILLIAM ADLINGTON, 1566)

tabooed shrine at Kildare. Like the Vestal Virgins of Rome who guarded the sacred flame, the priestesses of her shrine kept a perpetual fire burning there—a clear, bright flame worthy of a pure, shining goddess.

In Gaelic Scotland, Brigit was called Bride of the Golden Hair, Bride of the White Hills, Mother of the King of Glory, and was symbolized as a white swan. For the people of the Hebrides, Brigit was the goddess of childbirth.

Heavenly Muses

In her role as Muse, Brigit was the goddess who inspired poetry, and, according to medieval poets, the Virgin Mary was able to perform similar wonders: for them, she was guardian of the Cauldron of Inspiration. This cauldron was a powerful Celtic symbol, the fount of all knowingness, which traditionally belonged to the Goddess Cerridwen. Three drops of the magic brew it contained were sufficient to enlighten and inspire her son Taliesin, Chief of the Bards. In Irish poetry of the Middle Ages, Brigit and Mary were again linked for "Saint" Brigit was popularly known as "Mary of the Gael."

Brigit was also identified with the Carthaginian Tanit, Heavenly Goddess, and the Roman Juno Regina, Queen of Heaven—an epithet later inherited by the Christian Mary.

WELCOMING THE GODDESS

Various magical rituals were once enacted to mark and encourage the revival of vegetation at Imbolc, and to greet the Goddess who brought fertility with her. In Ireland and the Highlands of Scotland, she was accorded the following welcoming ceremony.

First, the mistress and servants of the house would

The Goddess (or priestess surrogate) from Crete, c. 1600 B.C. The snakes' renewal of themselves by shedding their skins symbolizes her power over life and death. The lion cub on her head shows she is Queen of the Animals, while the net pattern on her skirt suggests the web of life which she weaves.

ake a sheaf of oats, then dress it in women's clothes and lay it in a large basket, known as Briid's Bed, placing a club next to it. Before retiring, they would chant together three times, "Briid is come, Briid is welcome." If, in the morning, the impression of Briid's club was found in the ashes of the fire, it was deemed that crops would be plentiful in the year to come; if there was no impression, however, it was taken as a bad omen.

In other variations, a bed might be made from corn and hay, then covered with blankets and placed near the door. When the bed was ready, one of the occupants of the house would go outside and call three times, "Bridget, Bridget, come in, thy bed is ready"—an invitation to the Goddess to enter the home and fill the empty bed. Candles would be left burning near the bed all night.

In the Isle of Man, a festival known as *Laa'l Breeshey* was held on the eve of February 1. In this, the custom was for someone to stand by the door holding a bundle of green rushes, and, with the following words, invite Brigit to come in and lodge in the house that night:

"Brede, Brede, tar gys my thie tar dyn thie ayms noght. Foshil jee yn dorrys da Brede, as lhig da Brede e heet staigh."

Corn and rushes, ashes and flame—these are all emblems appropriate to Brigit, goddess of fertility and fire. The sheaf and bunch of greenery used in these rituals are reminiscent of the corn dolly that contains the Corn Spirit or Spirit of Vegetation, while the house fire and candles recall the sacred, ever-burning flame of Briigit's shrine. Traditionally, fire is also a symbol of prosperity and well-being (hence the old Scottish blessing, "Lang may yer lum reek," or "Long may your chimney smoke"), so the emphasis on fire in these rituals may reflect a belief in the house-spirit, the guardian of the home that resides in the very heart of it—the hearth—and whose element is the perpetual flame.

MAGIC CANDLES

The blessing of candles in church and the candlelit procession at the beginning of February has a pagan precedent: in ancient Rome, a similar rite at this time of year honored the goddess Juno Februata. It was this Juno who generated the *febris* (Latin for fever and the origin of the month's name) of love, and on this day, her worshippers carried burning candles around with them.

FIRE FESTIVAL

The old ways die hard, and candles continued to be used in English churches at Candlemas long after the Reformation and the rise of Protestantism, with its dislike of showy ceremonial. In 1628, the Bishop of Durham seriously annoyed the authorities with a display of pagan magnitude—at the Feast of the Purification, he had what amounted to a fire festival in his cathedral. ...the number of candles burnt that evening was two hundred and twenty, besides sixteen torches; sixty of those burning tapers and torches standing upon and near the high Altar.

Sacred water was one medium through which the Goddess—whether Brigit or Mary—could offer her healing magic. Here at Holywell in Cheshire, a religious complex grew up around the sacred waters.

INSET: An inscription of 1831 attests to the curative properties of one particular holy well.

T. M. Carew – Esqr.
Meath – west –
Cured Here Octr 1831.

ATHER

Even after Christianity was well established, people all over Europe still believed in the magical powers of candles blessed at the Feast of the Purification. According to old tradition in parts of France, these candles were kept and relit in times of sickness or storm; in the Tyrol, they were similarly lighted at the onset of a storm, or at important family occasions such as christenings or funerals; in Sicily, they were lit when there was an earthquake, or when someone was dying.

HEALING WATERS

If fire was one of the sacred elements of Brigit's Holy Trinity, so water was the element of the goddess's persona as healer. Water is the essential fluid that nurtures and nourishes all life—many an old tale tells of the quest to some outlandish spot, perhaps as far as the World's End, in search of the Water of Life—the magical *uschabheagh* of the Gaels—to cure the ailing king who represents the sickness of the land. There is also the well-known German story of Rapunzel, who cured her lover's blindness by watering his eyes with her tears. Think, too, of the scores of Christian pilgrims who still make the journey to the spring at Lourdes in south-west France to be cured of disabilities and illnesses by its sacred waters. This miraculous spring appeared at the same time as a series of visitations by the Virgin Mary to a peasant girl, Bernadette Soubirous, later St. Bernadette, as late as 1858—proof of the enduring belief in water as mystical healer.

But water is more than just a healing fluid—for the ancients, it was the very source of life itself, a primordial female element contained in such womb-symbols as well, font, and cauldron. The well is a particularly potent image, for in this the water erupts directly from the deep belly of the Earth.

The healing and life-giving powers of water are magical. Brigit's Aegean prototype seems to have been a moon goddess by the name of Brizo, derived from the Greek *brizein*, meaning to enchant. Our word "enchant" is derived from the Latin *incantare*, to sing, and thus literally means to spell-bind with singing, like a mother crooning a child to sleep with a lullaby, or a siren luring sailors to their deaths with her irresistible song. Water, healing, magic, and poetry all come together in the old custom of invoking Brigit's aid with poetic incantation by the side of holy wells, thus appealing to the goddess as both magical healer and muse.

As so often happens, clues to the past are discernible today, and wells sacred to Brigit may be traced simply through their names. In Ireland, there are St. Brigid's Wells at Killinagh in County Cavan, at Liscannor in County Clare, and at Cullienmore in Westmeath; there is also *Tobar Bhride*, or Bride's Well, in Roscommon, and in London Bridewell, the old women's prison, was originally a nunnery of St. Brigit.

People visited these holy wells to receive the benefits of their healing waters at auspicious times of the year—the pagan festivals of Imbolc, Beltane, Midsummer, Lughnasadh, and Samhain. The ritual might involve decorating the well with flowers and greenery, drinking the waters, and walking around the well-always *deiseil*, or sunways, never *widdershins*, or anti-clockwise, for this would bring bad luck.

MULTIPLE MAGIC

In Cornwall it was believed that a scald or burn could be healed by invoking the power of the triple Brigit. While chanting the rhyme:
Three Ladies came from the East,
One with fire and two with frost.
Out with thee, fire, and in with thee, frost.
Nine bramble leaves were dipped in spring water and applied to the scalded part. For the charm to work, it had to be repeated three times with each leaf. In this way, three—the magical number of the Goddess's trinity—was multiplied by another three to make nine, which was then multiplied by three again, magnifying the power of the spell twenty-seven times. Bramble is a plant sacred to the Triple Goddess, and the Three Ladies with their gifts represent the seasons, the cold freshness of virginal spring, the heat of full-blown summer, and the cold, old age of winter.

A DIVINE CURE

Where the marvels of modern medicine fail, the ancient healing powers of the Goddess still triumph, as in this story of a mother and her sick daughter, recorded by Lady Gregory in Galway, Ireland, in the early twentieth century:
"I brought my little girl that was not four years old to Saint Brigit's well on the cliffs, where she was ailing and pining away. I brought her as far as the doctors in Gort and they could do nothing for her and then I promised to go to Saint Brigit's well, and from the time that I made that promise she got better....
I made a promise to go to the well every year after that, and so I do ...And I brought a bottle of water from it last year and it is as cold as amber yet."

(LADY GREGORY, 1852-1932)

VALENTINE'S DAY

Oft have I heard both youths and virgins say
Birds choose their mates and couple, too, today
But by their flight I never can divine
When I shall couple with my Valentine.
(*HESPERIDES*, ROBERT HERRICK, 1648)

Fourteen days after Imbolc people all over the world celebrate Valentine's Day. According to tradition, this is the day when the birds choose their mates for the year. It is also the day for the blossoming of love between young women and men, and so introduces the theme of love-making and magical fertility rites that begins in February, and gathers in strength throughout Spring, continuing right through to May Day.

In the cold north, when the Earth is only just beginning to shake off the enchanted sleep of Winter, it may seem a little soon for such erotic fancies. However, it must be remembered that many of the festivals we now honor have their origins in the Near East and Mediterranean—the homeland of the Romans who spread their influence across all Europe—and here the seasons come earlier. Changes in the calendar have shifted dates, too, so that festivals that may seem more appropriate to a particular period fall in another.

Valentine's Day is named after a Christian saint, but just who he was is not clear, for there is more than one contender for the title. One Valentine was a Roman priest who was imprisoned for helping persecuted Christians, and who became a Christian himself. Although he restored the sight of his jailer's blind daughter, he was still martyred, being brutally clubbed to death on February 14, 269. Another Valentine was also a Christian martyr who, before his death, scratched a message to his beloved on the wall of his cell, ending with the words "Your Valentine."

As a festival of love, Valentine's Day has powerful associations with two Roman love fests. The first is the sacred day of Juno Februata, the patroness of the "fever" of love, at the beginning of February, mentioned earlier. Then, on February 15, there is the Lupercalia, a festival of purification and fertility in honor of Faunus, or Lupercus, a rustic fertility god. This feast was later

An elaborate Victorian Valentine's card. Such demure messages of love, traditionally sent on February 14, are a pale echo of the "fever" of love once celebrated in ancient Rome with the first stirring of Spring.

The thoughts of love first engendered in February become stronger as spring progresses. In this illumination from a French "shepherd's calendar" of c. 1495, showing Aries the Ram and Taurus the Bull from the latter part of springs, a lover bears flowers to his lady.

suppressed by Pope Gelasius in 494 A.D., and replaced with the celebration in honor of the Purification of the Virgin—the modern Candlemas which now falls on February 2.

During Juno Februata's orgiastic revels, the young men of Rome would draw "billets," small slips of paper naming their female partners. This finds echoes in an old English Valentine's Day custom whereby lots would be drawn to discover one's "valentine," and the chosen one would then be given a gift, often a pair of gloves.

In this season of Virgin Goddesses, Brides and Love, it is only natural that young unmarried women should find they have special privileges. According to an old British custom, any village girl could, on leaving her home on the morning of Valentine's Day, hail the first young marriageable man she met with the following binding words:

Good morrow Valentine, I go today,
To wear for you what you must pay,
A pair of gloves next Easter Day.

LOVE CHARMS

With thoughts of love and marriage uppermost in their minds, young women would indulge in a little divination as to their future partners on Valentine's Day. One method open to the more brave-hearted was to slip into the churchyard at night, and run around the church three times (or twelve times), scattering hemp seed between the graves as they ran, and singing:

I sow hemp seed,
Hemp seed I sow.
Come my true love,
Follow and mow.

If the magic worked, the young women would see the shadowy forms of their future husbands following behind them, picking up the seed.

Another, less demanding custom involved floating three apples—fruits of wisdom, sacred marriage, and eternal life—in a bowl of water. Then, having taken her shoes off and placed them in a T shape, the inquirer would chant the following charm three times:

I place my shoes like the letter T,
In hopes my true love I shall see,
In his apparel and his array
As he is now and every day.

After this, she would go to bed, leaving letters written on pieces of paper to float face down on the water overnight. In the morning, most of these scraps would have sunk, and on those that had turned over on the bottom of the bowl she would see the initials or name of her future husband.

CHAPTER 5

THE SACRED MARRIAGE
MARCH 21: THE SPRING EQUINOX

...and the desert shall rejoice, and blossom
as the rose....
Then shall the lame man leap as an hart,
and the tongue of the dumb sing: for in the
wilderness shall waters break out, and streams
in the desert. And the parched ground shall
become a pool and the thirsty land springs of
water: in the habitation of dragons, where
each lay, shall be grass with reeds
and rushes.

(ISAIAH, CHAPTER 35, VERSE 6)

The Spring Equinox celebrates both Earth and Sun, both growth and light. At this point in the solar calendar, the length of daylight equals the length of the night—the male Sun balances the female Moon. After the Equinox, the balance will shift in favor of the growing Sun as he begins to make the day longer than the night. Four days later in the Old Style calendar, March 25, was New Year's Day .

In the lunar calendar that relates to the seasons, the Equinox also signals an important phase for the female Earth for this is the time that she opens herself, ready to receive new seed and to bring forth the plant life that has overwintered inside her. The month of April, which arrives shortly after the Equinox, derives its name from the Latin *aperio*, to open (as in the word aperture). In Moon symbolism, Imbolc represents the New Moon, and the Spring Equinox is the Waxing Moon.

Christ's Springtime "rebirth," painted by Raphael c. 1499. Notice the three women behind him, traditionally the Virgin Mary, Mary Magdalene, and Mary, mother of James. Their number recalls the Goddess's trinity.

For the Anglo-Saxons April was *Eostramonath*, after their goddess Eoestre. Like her Greek counterpart Eos or Aurora—who left her marital bed at the end of each night and rose from the ocean, lighting the dark sky with her rosy fingers—Eoestre brought the dawn of the day. In April, she also brings the dawn of the year.

Eoestre gave her name to Easter, which in the Christian faith replaced the Jewish Passover or "Pesach" (*Pascha* in Latin). This movable feast, which commemorates the resurrection of Jesus, is fixed according to the patterns of the Moon, falling the first Sunday following the first Full Moon after the Spring Equinox.

THE SACRED MARRIAGE

At the Spring Equinox, different threads from the solar and seasonal calendars are woven together into a single strand. At this time of year, daylight is equal to darkness, so the God and Goddess make a well-matched couple. In the seasonal cycle, the Earth has released the plant life that has lain dormant within her through the dark days of winter—in other words, the Green Man, the spirit of vegetation, has returned. He is the "son", or a reincarnation of, the Corn King cut down at the last harvest. As well as releasing this spirit of plant life, however, the Earth is also ready to receive new seed, and this is where the two cycles meet. The Spring Equinox—being the turning point at which the light is about to overtake the dark—is the obvious moment for the Goddess to conceive the next sun child, to be born in nine months' time at the Winter Solstice. The Equinox may therefore be seen as the time of renewal in the widest sense, for there is both conception and (re)birth. Now the Goddess mates with her lover-son-lover, to conceive her next son, in an eternally repeating cycle.

What sounds like a pattern of incest in fact has more in common with the old right of succession of kings, and what was known as the "sacred marriage." In the ancient world, the power on the throne was female—sovereignty was invested in the queen, and did not pass down through the male line. A man assumed the honor of kingship only by marriage to the queen, and she did the choosing. She was the earthly representative of the Goddess, and so union with her was sacred; it was truly "holy matrimony."

Like the Goddess, however, the queen had a darker side to her erotic personality—what she loved she could destroy, what she gave life to she could take life from. If the king lost his appeal or outlived his appointed hour, he could be disposed of: if he was lucky, he might be banished; if less fortunate, death was his fate. His murder was often a necessary ritual so that he, the "father," might make way for his successor, the "son."

The theme of the sacred marriage and the pattern of lover-son-lover is seen everywhere—in historical practice, in myth, and, of course, in the union between the Goddess and her God. For the God, love and death are two sides of the same coin, his *liebestod*, "love-death." After his allotted span as consort, the God must die so that his essence can be reabsorbed back into the Earth to maintain her continued fertility: the father must make way for the son. In classical mythology, this idea is represented in the story of Oedipus, the "son" of Jocasta, who murdered his "father," Laius, to marry his mother (used in Freudian psychology as a model for a boy's incestuous yearnings for his mother).

Among the priesthood of the mortals, high priestesses enacted the magical marriage rites of the God and her lover with a chosen surrogate—a youth decked and decorated for this high honor who, after copulation, would be sacrificed. Later, ways were found to kill the God—surrogate only symbolically. In Ireland, ancient kings "married the land," embodied in the queen—and in Northern Europe, woe betide any king if the land proved infertile. This would be taken as sign that his virility, and therefore his usefulness, was waning.

THE HUSBANDS OF QUEEN MAB

The right of kingly succession was an old and honorable tradition, and was seen as such by no less a personage than the Fairy Queen herself, who embraced the concept with whole-hearted enthusiasm. Bored with her husband King Conchobar, the mythological Irish Queen Medb of Connacht—the very embodiment of sovereignty—discarded him to bestow her favours on various men including Tinde, Eochaid Dála, and Aillall mac Máta, all of whom became kings of Connacht. The Queen was spoilt for choice for there were other suitors, too—in fact, it is said that she never had one man without another waiting in his shadow. Her namesake, Queen Medb Lethberg of Leinster, was similarly energetic, marrying what amounted to a dynasty of no fewer than nine kings of Ireland in succession. So great was her power that she would not allow a man to become king unless he became her husband.

THE PREGNANT VIRGIN

And the angel said unto her, Fear not, Mary: for thou hast found favour with God. And behold, thou shalt conceive in thy womb, and bring forth a son, and shalt call his name Jesus ... then said Mary unto the angel, How shall this be, seeing I know not a man? And the angel answered and said unto her, The Holy Ghost shall come upon thee, and the power of the Highest shall overshadow thee: therefore also that holy thing which shall be born of thee shall be called the Son of God.
(ST. LUKE, CHAPTER 1, VERSES 30-35)

Around the Spring Equinox is a period of special celebration for Christians, too, who also remember the conception of their God and his resurrection at this time of year. The rich wellsprings that nourished the old pagan religions of the Middle East and Mediterranean fed the new Christianity as well, and both share the same archetypes. A look at the mysteries of the Christian Spring provides a peephole into the ancient symbolism of this season.

Four days after the Equinox, March 25, is Lady Day or the Feast of the Annunciation (the Old Style date was April 6). By tradition, this is the day when the Archangel Gabriel appeared to Mary to tell her she was to conceive the child that will be born at the Winter Solstice, and who will be known as the Light of the World. The beloved Virgin finds that she is to become the mother of God (the Son) and therefore the bride of God (the Father). Her son will later be sacrificed and reborn. In other words, she is following the time-

THE PRINCESS IN THE FOREST OF THORNS

The much-loved story of the Sleeping Beauty has been so dulled by familiarity that we may no longer be able to feel its magic and sense its meaning. Looked at through fresh eyes, however, it reveals itself as a nature myth rich in metaphor.

At the princess's first birthday feast, she is cursed by an uninvited guest, the thirteenth Wise Woman, who says that when she reaches the age of fifteen, she will prick her finger on a spindle and die. The numbers involved here are all highly symbolic. Thirteen is a Moon number—the number of months in a lunar year—while fifteen is three times five, five being a number sacred to the Goddess (as in the five-pointed pentacle), and three representing the main phases of the Moon (Waxing, Full, and Waning), the Ages of Woman (Virgin, Mother, and Crone), and the seasons of Spring, Summer and Autumn. Thus, at fifteen, the princess will already have passed through her first three "ages," and be ready for her fourth and final phase that will complete the cycle—Winter and the Dark Moon.

The story facilitates her progress by allowing the princess, as prophesied, to prick her finger on a phallic spindle. The spindle is offered to her at the top of the tower by an unknown old woman, clearly the thirteenth Wise Woman returned with her spinning wheel of destiny and her thread of wyrd to seal the heroine's fate.

The injury does not, however, lead to death, but to a still and death-like slumber, for the curse has been softened by another faery woman. Prepared for later fertility by the pricking of the spindle, the Sleeping Beauty—like the Dormant Earth containing seeds—now succumbs to apparent lifelessness. As she does so, so does every single living thing around her, from the flies on the wall to the leaves on the trees, freezing in the position they were at that moment, while an impenetrable forest of thorns springs up around the wintry palace.

Finally, a hundred years later, the moment of regeneration comes. The magical forest parts to allow through the lover-prince who will trigger Nature's awakening with a kiss. In this moment, as male is united with female, all that seemed dead now bursts with new life. Spring and the world have woken.

The sleep and awakening of the sleeping Beauty may be used as a nature myth, the princess's waking signifying the coming Spring.

honored pattern familiar the length and breadth of the ancient world from at least as early as 5,500 B.C.—that of the Goddess who is the mother-bride of the son-lover God, who will die and will live again.

Mary is naturally surprised at the news of her forthcoming pregnancy because she "knows not a man." The angel reassures her, and tells her that she will conceive in suitably mystical fashion as befits the Mother of God (*Panagia Theotokus* in Greek, as her official title was after A.D. 431.) Divine conception need not depend on the usual biological method which is the sole option for mortals. Depending on where the Goddess is in her various stages of evolution, she can create life all by herself, she can conceive by means of some mystical union, or she can openly consort with the God in sacred love-making.

Pagan religion abounds with images of magical conceptions. In ancient Asia Minor, Nana, an earthly incarnation of the mother goddess Cybele, conceived Attis by eating an almond or a pomegranate. Meanwhile, in Rome, the goddess Juno Februata became pregnant with the god Mars through mystical union with a flower—her sacred lily, later the Easter Lily of the Virgin Mary. In classical Greece, Danaë was locked away by her father to prevent her from bearing a son who would kill him, as the oracle had foretold. However, she conceived the divine hero Perseus when Zeus—metamorphosed into his essence, a shower of "golden rain"—poured himself into her womb. Still trying to avert his fate, Danaë's father bound his daughter and grandson in a chest and cast it on the waves, from which they were eventually delivered, caught in the nets of a fisherman—Perseus' "second birth."

Further north, there are myths of similarly miraculous conceptions. Although the Irish hero Cú Chulainn was said to be the son of the shining god Lugh, the actual cause of his birth—the generative principle—was a mayfly swallowed by his mother Dechtire, according to one version of the story. In Britain, the goddess Cerridwen bore the divine bard Taliesin after swallowing the single grain into which her servant boy, Gwion Bach, had transformed himself.

Arianrhod, the Celtic equivalent of Nana and Ariadne, was a most unwilling mother. When her virginity, of which the maiden was sure, was put to the test by the great magician Math, the boy Dylan Eil Ton, Twin of the

MAKING THE WORLD GO ROUND

The timing of Mary's "union" with God on March 25 finds parallels in the Springtime sacred marriages of Dumuzi to Inanna in Sumeria, and their counterparts Tammuz to Ishtar in Babylonia. Such was the importance of these divine pairings that they initiated the beginning of the New Year: in former Christian times, March 25 was one of the days designated New Year's Day, while the lovemaking of Inanna-Ishtar and Dumuzi-Tammuz set off the year in their respective cultures.

APRIL FOOLS

Twelve o'clock is past and gone, You're the fool for making me one.

The first day of April is a traditional day for tricks and pranks, but only until noon. It has the features of the kind of feast of misrule that attends major "cracks" in the year, as the rule of the old disintegrates into chaos to be reformed into order by the rule of the new.

Wave, unexpectedly dropped from her womb. Arianrhod was to conceive unknowingly again. In the chaos that ensued after the emergence of Dylan, the goddess did not notice another mysterious form falling from her body—a small germ of life—but Math did. He seized the secret object, wrapped it in a cloth, and hid it in a casket, where he tended it with his magic arts, like a physician nurturing an embryo in a tube. The end result was Llew Llaw Gyffes, the Fair-haired One with the Sure Hand.

THE CHILD FROM THE SEA

In Mary's case, God the Father impregnates her "in spirit" via his middle persona, a Holy Ghost. According to the creed "conceived by the Holy Ghost," Jesus already exists in embryo in God's spirit, his divine mind, but needs fleshing out to become God the Man—and Mary's earthly body is the vehicle that the Father has chosen for this purpose.

God's spirit is that same force that "moved on the face of the waters" in the Old Testament to create the world out of the formless void, and so suggests another of Mary's faces—that of Goddess of the Sea in whose watery womb Jesus grows. Dressed in her traditional blue cloak and white gown, Mary wears the colors of wave and foam, while her halo of stars brings to mind her other title, the Latin *Stella Maris*, or Star of the Sea, by which Isis, Ishtar, Venus, and Aphrodite were also known. This last was also referred to as "Mari," the Sea, and the name Mary has been linked with the Latin *mare*, meaning sea. Even that sea-temptress the mermaid has similar linguistic roots, for her name was once written "merry-maid." As if piecing together fragments of memory, Mediterranean peoples continue to honor Mary as Goddess of the Sea. On special occasions, her effigy is set in a small boat and comes floating over the waves to greet the faithful, just as the joyful Love Goddess Aphrodite, with her seashell, once arose from the wine-dark waters of the Deep.

Thus, as the vessel that gives flesh to the Son of God, Mary is matter, the stuff of Earth; but she is also the Sea, eternal, deep beyond the measure of man, solid yet fluid, endlessly in flux, governed by the Moon. Born of and personifying the Deep, Mary-Aphrodite gives birth from her own waters.

In this richly meaningful Christian picture, we see the eternal symbols that have lain embedded for millennia deep in the human psyche, but have here been reassembled in a new patchwork image to align with the message of Christianity.

The story of Christ's conception has stimulated much controversy. Literal, rational thinkers point out the absurdity of procreation without sexual intercourse. Feminists make a similar point, that Mary embodies a traditional male ideal of womanhood by being submissive and devoid of sexuality. Even some members of the modern clergy have rejected the concept of the "Immaculate" Conception. Ironically, this is where pagan models can come to the rescue, giving a deeper insight into this seemingly paradoxical mystery.

In the Christian version of the story, Mary has a totally passive role. She is no more than a medium chosen by God the Father to give physical form to God the Son—rather like the wood or stone a sculptor might use to express an idea already formed in his head. Here, in giving her such secondary status, the patriarchal imperative has turned the old pagan model on its head in order to give a male god total power of procreation. When we approach the story from a different viewpoint, however, we see that Mary and all the other "virgin mothers" mentioned earlier are not secondary figures at all—quite the reverse, in fact. In each example, it is the mother with her solid, physical reality who is central and who therefore assumes the major role in the mystery of conception and birth; the father, on the other hand, is peripheral, distant, often invisible, making contact with the mother at most in symbolic form. While the mother is present, the father is absent.

Viewed in this light, the story takes on a completely different meaning. Now we see that Mary and all her virgin sisters are none other than evolutions of the great Stone Age Mother Goddess who did not need the services of a man to conceive. Far from being a rejection of the feminine, the Immaculate Conception and Virgin Birth instead become triumphs for Woman, who stands—as she always has—at the epicenter of Creation.

THE COMING OF TALIESIN

In a place as high as the highest hill and deep as the deepest valley, there once lived a great and powerful sorceress named Cerridwen. Now this Cerridwen had a little son who went by the name of Afagddu and he was the ugliest boy in all the world, and almost the stupidest, too. About his looks his mother could do little, but about his knowledge—well, there she could take a hand. So Cerridwen turned to her books of faery arts, and pored long and hard over the pages, until at last she discovered a spell for making a Cauldron of Inspiration. It had to boil for a year and a day, after which whoever tasted the first three drops of its magic brew would know all that there is to know.

Cerridwen began to make the magic potion. Into her Cauldron she poured herbs and spices and other precious things, as well as the red berries called *borfes y Gwion*. She stirred her Cauldron and set it a-bubbling, then she placed her servant boy, Gwion Bach, by it to tend it for a year and a day.

Morning, noon and night the boy watched the Cauldron, stirring it and keeping it boiling. But then, when the year and a day was nearly done, three small drops of the brew splashed onto Gwion Bach's fingers and he licked them—and in that instant, he knew all that there was to know in the past, the present, and the future. And one of the things he knew was that his Mistress was going

to kill him. He jumped up, and the Cauldron shattered
because all the brew that remained in it was a deadly poison.
And Gwion Bach ran and he ran, with Cerridwen chasing
after him. He changed himself into a hare, but Cerridwen
became a hound, and the chase went on. He changed himself
into a fish, but Cerridwen became an otter, and the chase
went on. He changed himself into a dove, but Cerridwen
became a hawk, and
the chase went on. He changed himself into a grain of wheat,
and Cerridwen became a black hen. And the black hen
pecked about among the wheat until she found the one grain
that was Gwion Bach, and she ate him up.

And time passed, and in the passing of nine months
Cerridwen bore another son, and this son was called Gwion.
Now Cerridwen would ordinarily have killed the unwanted
baby, but he was so beautiful that even she shrank from this
cruelty. So, instead of killing him then and there, she placed
him inside a skin bag, and threw him into the sea to take
his luck.

The skin bag floated off on the waves, and sailed the seas for
many a year, with the baby inside growing in age not one day
older. And at last, one May Eve when the time was right, the
bag was caught in the nets of King Gwyddno, that were set to
snare the salmon, magical fish of knowledge.

On this day, the King had given the rights to empty the nets
to his son Elphin. And the first thing that Elphin found in the
nets was not a salmon, but a treasure much greater … for
when he opened the bag, out burst a child speaking words of
magic and radiant as the Sun, so that Elphin called him
Taliesin, meaning
"Shining Brow."

And when Taliesin came into the great hall of the King, these
were his words of greeting:
I am Taliesin
I sing perfect metre which will last till the world's end
I know why an echo answers again
why liver is bloody, why breath is black and why silver shines
I know why a cow has horns
and why a woman loves a man
why milk is white and holly green
ale bitter and ocean brine
how many spears make a confrontation
how many drops a shower of rain
I know why there are scales on fish and black feet on swans
I have been a blue salmon
a dog, a stag, a roebuck on the mountain
a stock, a spade, an axe in the hand
a buck, a bull, a stallion
upon a hill I was grown as grain
reaped and in the oven thrown
out of that roasting I fell to the ground
pecked up and swallowed by the
black hen
in her crop nine nights lain
I have been dead, I am alive, I am Taliesin.

(Cerridwen was a Celtic goddess, and Taliesin's attributes of
"shining brow" and his way with words make him a Celtic Apollo,
Greek God of the Sun and Poetry; he also had a sixth-century
namesake, the Welsh bard Taliesin. The various forms Gwion-
Taliesin took, and his death-rebirth process, may reflect the
changes of the seasons.)

THE DEAD AND RISEN GOD

The most appropriate time for the God to die would seem to be at harvest, when he has ripened from the virile Green Man of Spring into the gloriously golden John Barleycorn of Autumn. This is the pattern followed by such divine figures as the Sumerian Dumuzi, beloved of Inanna, and their Babylonian counterparts, Tammuz and Ishtar. Some Green Men, however, suffer this fate in Spring—as if the Earth needs an extra boost of their magical blood now to assist in the processes of growth.

Like Tammuz-Dumuzi, who are hacked to death with sickles, their death, too, is violent. After a farewell love-making session with Aphrodite, Adonis, whose name means "Lord," was killed, castrated by the horns of a boar. Wherever his blood touched the Spring soil, red anemones sprang up.

Around the Spring Equinox in Rome, worshippers honored the passion of Attis, beloved of Cybele. Great Goddess of all Asia Minor, Cybele had arrived in the city in 204 B.C., where her temple stood on the site of the present-day St. Peter's. From Rome her worship spread through the Empire, across Europe.

Like Adonis, Cybele's lover was castrated. On March 15, the reeds that embodied his spirit were cut and carried in procession through the city. On March 22, he was again "killed" as if on the altar of the Goddess herself—an undying, evergreen pine was felled in Cybele's sacred grove, then bound with cloth and adorned with violets, the flower that was said to have sprung up from Attis' blood like the anemones of Adonis. On March 24, the Day of Blood, his death was mourned and the *Taurobolium*, the sacrifice of a bull, took place, its genitals given as a sacred offering to the Goddess. At the end of the day an overnight watch began, for it was known that Attis, having given himself in sacrifice to the Goddess, would rise again from the tomb in which he was buried. In the morning of March 25, the high priest announced to the people that they were saved, for the God was risen. This day was the *Hilaria*, a festival of joy and revelry of all kinds in honor of the reborn God. (When Julius Caesar later altered the calendar, the *Hilaria* and its rites, which were celebrated all over Europe, moved from March 25 to May 1.)

Cybele in her lion-drawn chariot faces her son-lover Attis, here in his role as the
"good shepherd" with his crook. The vine and horn of wheat are emblems of the
vegetation god.

THE ORDEAL OF ODIN

Although Odin—supreme king and magician-god of the Norsepeople—was not associated with the fertility of the Earth, he nevertheless chose a similar mode of death to other sacrificial gods on the tree, or in the tree. Odin knew that in dying he would live, so he "consecrated himself to himself," in a similar rite to that between God the Son and God the Father. Wounding himself with his own spear, Odin set himself to hang on the "windy tree"—the great ash Yggdrasil whose roots, trunk, and branches form the entire world. For nine nights the God remained hanging, bleeding, buffeted by storm and without food or drink, until at last he noticed some runes—magic letters first possessed by the goddess Idun, keeper of the apples of immortality—engraved on stone below him. Summoning up the last drop of his strength, slowly and painfully he managed to lift the runes—and was immediately released from his self-imposed ordeal, and filled with new life and vigor.

Echoes of Attis' ritual murder are found in the death of Cú Chulainn, who was bound to a pillar and shot at with arrows, the blood from his wounds flowing down to redden the Earth, and in the passion of Jesus Christ.

The conception, death and resurrection of Jesus that is celebrated all over the Christian world at this time of year reveals a wealth of magical symbolism, combining features of both solar and lunar-seasonal calendars with ancient pagan imagery. Jesus has features of both Sun God and Green Man. The date of the Annunciation is solar, as befits a conquering god of light who will triumph over darkness. His death and resurrection, however, reflect the phases of the Moon and the patterns of seasonal growth. Good Friday, when he is buried, and Easter, when he rises, are fixed according to a lunar date. His conception-death-resurrection is entirely fitting for the Spring Equinox period, for until the calendar change in 1752 this was the New Year—his death is the dying of old time, his conception-resurrection the birth of new time.

Knowing that he must die, Jesus invites his Apostles to a ritual, a Last Supper. Here he offers himself in holy sacrifice, and his companions partake of its power, eating his body and drinking his blood (as did the followers of Attis and Dionysus) from a sacred chalice, the Holy Grail. The Lord then suffers a brutal death on a tree-shaped cross, after which his disciples anoint his body with spices, wrap it in "linen clothes," and bury it in a sepulcher. When they return three days later, they find the stone rolled away from the entrance, the body gone, and an angel who asks them, "Why seek ye the living amongst the dead?"

The three days Jesus has spent in the tomb, or Underworld, echo the three days of the Dark Moon, the equivalent of Winter when all life sleeps. The "tree" on which he died turns out to have been a Tree of Life, like the undying pine of Attis, for the Lord is not dead but risen. A miracle has happened. The One-that-died has been reborn, bringing with him light, life and salvation.

Christ's death, on a "tree," and his resurrection at the time of year when nature is reviving, has many pagan echoes.

EASTER FOOD

Hot Cross Buns, Hot Cross Buns,
One a penny, two a penny,
Hot Cross Buns;
If you have no daughters,
Give them to your sons,
One a penny, two a penny,
Hot Cross Buns.

On "God's Friday" or Good Friday, it is the custom in Britain to eat round, spicy, fruit-filled buns, known as hot cross buns, with a cross decoration on top. Although this is said to represent the Crucifix on which Christ died, its arms are of equal length, unlike the long-tailed Latin or Passion Cross adopted by Christianity, although this was not fully accepted as a religious symbol by the Christian Church until the ninth century.

The cross is a very old and universal motif with many meanings. The combination of cross and round bun recalls the Celtic Cross, or Hindu *kiakra*, which represented the union of male and female—the phallic cross within the yonic circle—which would be appropriate for this Springtime sacred marriage.

The hot cross buns of Good Friday may be descendants of the cakes offered by the Greeks to the goddesses Artemis and Hecate and the Moon. These cakes were round, symbolizing the Full Moon, and were decorated with "horns" that formed a cross-shape and represented the four quarters of the lunar cycle.

The egg, now of chocolate, that we eat on Easter Sunday—the "Sun's Day" when the Light of the World was reborn—is the ultimate symbol of female fertility. In old Russia, it was the custom to place Easter eggs on graves as magic resurrection charms. These were colored red, for Life and life's-blood. In Germany on the eve of Easter Day, children were told to be good so that the "hare" would lay eggs for them, thus making a link between egg, Easter Bunny, and Easter goddess. The Hare was the Moon's sacred animal in both East and West, and Eoestre was a northern form of Astarte who, in Egyptian tradition, was said to have laid the Golden Egg of the Sun.

ABOVE: In an English church, Easter flowers adorn the baptismal font, the "womb" of water from which Christian children are "born again."

OPPOSITE: The Celtic Cross combines the "tree" emblem of the dead and risen God and the circle of the Goddess.

CHAPTER 6

LORD OF THE GREENWOOD AND QUEEN OF THE MAY

MAY 1: BELTANE

And thus it passed on from Candlemass until after Easter, that the month of May was come, when every lusty heart beginneth to blossom, and to bring forth fruit; for like as herbs and trees bring forth fruit and flourish in May, in likewise every lusty heart that is any manner a lover, springeth and flourisheth in lusty deeds.

(*LE MORTE D'ARTHUR*, SIR THOMAS MALORY, C. 1470)

May Eve, April 30, ushers in a most joyful season, as the month of May blossoms forth in all the flowers and greenery of late Spring and early Summer. This is the time to get up before dawn on May 1 to see the sun rise and to gather may—the flowering hawthorn—or perhaps birch or rowan; the time to wear green in honor of the verdant Earth; and, above all, the time to enjoy the pleasures of love.

The name "May" is thought to be derived from Maya or Maia, Goddess of Spring, and in Scandinavia the month is dedicated to Maj, the Maiden. In Saxon England, May was "Sproutkale," or "Tri-milchi" because at this time cows were said to be giving milk three times a day. The day that we call May Day and celebrate on May 1 would, because of alterations in the calendar, previously have fallen on May 13, which was May Day Old Style.

In an English village, dancing children with flowery garlands celebrate the coming of May.

In the Celtic calendar, May Eve was the start of one of the most important festivals of the year, the great feast of Beltane. The origins of the name are not clear. Some believe it derives from *bel-dine*, "dine" meaning cattle, because newborn cattle were sacrificed on this day to Bel or Bial, a Celtic Baal, counterpart to the Scandinavian Balder. Others believe that the name means bright fire, from *belos*, bright or shining, and *taine* or *tan*, fire. Either way, fire certainly formed a central part of the Beltane rituals—as it also did in later at Midsummer, the twin of this Maytime celebration.

THE ATTRACTION OF OPPOSITES

The Beltane revels share some of the character of the Spring Equinox earlier in the year—again there is a focus on the sacred marriage. This may partly be due to alterations in the calendar which moved the festivities of late March and early April forward to May, and also to climatic variations between southern and northern Europe. Spring and Summer come earlier in the south, so that a sacred marriage would naturally be celebrated earlier in the south than the north. As a Celtic festival, however, Beltane adds its own unique flavor to the union of the Goddess and God.

The Celts were fascinated with duality and alternating opposites—light and dark, night and day, life and death—and accordingly divided the year into two. Beltane was the feast that marked the end of the winter half (which in turn was halved by Imbolc, the start of Spring) and the beginning of summer. Samhain (Halloween)—Beltane's partner—brought the end of the Summer half and the beginning of Winter, as well as the beginning of the Celtic year. In many Romance tales, which have Celtic roots, Summer overtaking Winter was pictured as a contest between two rivals to win a desired Lady, a contest which often took place on May Eve or in the early part of May.

Beltane also has powerful associations with the Otherworld, of which more will be said in the following chapter.

THE BATTLE OF THE TWO SUITORS

In ancient Britain, Creiddylad, the daughter of Llud Llawereint, was betrothed to Gwythr, son of Greidawl. However, before the marriage could be consummated, the bride was borne off by Gwyn ap Nudd. When word of this outrage came to the ears of King Arthur, he commanded the thief to set Creiddylad free. A compromise, however, was reached. It was agreed that the bride would be returned to her father's house, where she would remain in peace while her two suitors competed for her hand. Accordingly, at the beginning of every May, Gwythr and Gwyn enter into battle with each other, and so they are fighting still, as they will until the world nears its end. Whoever is then the victor will win Creiddylad at last.

THE BATTLE OF THE SEASONS

Rivals in love were not the only ones to battle it out at Beltane. At this crucial turning point of the seasons, there was no reason why Winter should give way to Summer without a fight. Thus on May Day in many different corners of Europe the representative and followers of Winter, clad in fur and adorned with straw, entered into mock battle with the representative and troops of Summer, dressed in green or white and decked with flowers and leaves. Summer, of course, always won, and Winter's fate might include being stripped of his straw, ducked in the village well, or driven out into the forest.

THE ROYAL COUPLE

The central figure in the May Day celebrations is the May Queen, a girl specially chosen for the honor who, dressed in white and crowned with garlands of flowers, is carried in procession around the village. This flowery maiden is no mere bucolic beauty, however, but a representative of the Goddess that presides over this season of fruitfulness and fertility.

For the Anglo-Saxons, the May Bride was their Love Goddess, with her ancient association with the cult of the May tree. Across the water in Scandinavia, there was the great Norse Freya or Frigg, who included among her many attributes that of Goddess of Love and who paraded in May-Day processions under the guise of the partly clothed, partly naked "Lady Godiva." Further south in Rome there was Flora, Goddess of Spring—a lady of pleasure whose May Day festival, the Floralia, was marked by singing, dancing, and open-air revelry involving "licentious and promiscuous" behavior, according to Christian Church fathers. The May festivities of Northern Europe have also been linked with the cult of the Great Mother of the Mediterranean region, the Phrygian Cybele, patroness of "free love," whose great festival was the joyous Hilaria that celebrated the return of her lover, Attis.

The May Queen's mortal partner is a curious figure—a Green Man, Jack-in-the-Green, Leaf King, or Green George (abroad in old Russia on April 23) who appears smothered in a costume of leaves and perhaps encased in a cage

of branches or wicker. Emerging from the wildness of the wood, he personifies the spirit of vegetation. His enclosing framework of branches hints at what may once have been his fate, either real or symbolic. A "Green Man," made from a basket of leafy fronds, would once have been cast on to a bonfire as a sacrifice, to intensify the magic powers of death by flame. Such a "death" of the King is in accordance with the ancient custom of ritual regicide, in which the sacred king, consort of the Goddess's earthly representative, the queen, is killed by his successor.

UNDER THE GREENWOOD TREE

Greensleeves was all my joy,
Greensleeves was my delight,
Greensleeves was my heart of gold,
And who but Lady Greensleeves?
(A COURTLY SONNET FROM *A HANDFUL OF PLEASANT DELITES*, 1584)

At Beltane, male and female come together, whether they be God and Goddess or mere mortals. The May Queen and King embody the divine pair, whose sacred union ensures growth and fertility. In joyful celebration and imitation of the divine marriage, human beings, too, join together in their own union of love.

If May is the time for love, it is the extra-marital kind, however. In this case, love and marriage definitely do not go together—after all, the Love Goddess is hardly likely to follow convention, but goes where her heart and her passions lead her. May, then, is the merry month of elopements, of trysts, of illicit meetings in the greenwood. The concept of Romantic Love, of love for love's sake, was a plant foreign to the soil of northern Europe. It grew from a seed brought back from the East by returning Crusaders in the Middle Ages, and at the center of the cult was Woman as Goddess, a figure to be adored and worshipped, and attainable only for one worthy enough. The open-air freedoms of blossoming May and its associations with sensual and erotic pleasures, melded well with the Romantic ideal, and in the words of minstrel and bard this, *par excellence*, was the month to "make much joy"—and where

OPPOSITE: In May, Nature caresses the senses, and entices lovers out for assignations "beneath the greenwood tree."

better to make this joy than amidst the beauties of Nature?

For Welsh poets of the thirteenth and fourteenth centuries, May was the time for secret assignations in the "house of leaves," the lover's bower, which often stood below a birch tree or in a birch bush (reminders of these rendezvous were offered in the form of birch-wreath love tokens). That which is furthest from reach is often that which is most alluring, and women with the greatest powers of attraction were frequently married rather than single—whether they be the wives of flesh-and-blood men or, even more tantalizingly perhaps, the "brides of Christ" of the nunneries.

Going "a-maying"—visiting the greenwood to collect flowering hawthorn, or perhaps birch—became synonymous with the pleasures of love. In medieval times, ladies of the court and their knights would ride in pairs to the woods, led by the Queen of the May on a white horse and her male consort on a black one. Ordinary people, too, enjoyed such seasonal visits to the greenwood. On May Eve, large parties of both sexes would venture forth to gather May, and would spend the night outdoors, love-making among the trees.

The abandon of May was obviously at odds with settled conjugal life by the domestic hearth, and those who chose to wed now did so at their peril. It was said that marriages made in May would only last one summer, and an old Irish book of law even went so far as to cite Beltane as the most common time for divorce. In this month of love, it was the unloving and the unkind, not the unmarried, that were scorned. In parts of Wales, young men would fix beribboned bunches of flowers to the houses of the young women they loved; to those of prudes, however, or of women who had jilted their lovers, they attached a straw effigy of a man, or a horse's skull.

Married in May and kirked in green
Both bride and bridegroom won't
long be seen.

(TRADITIONAL SAYING)

O' marriages in May
Bairns die in decay.

(TRADITIONAL SAYING)

QUEEN OF THE GLADE

Medieval romance tells how different suitors vied for the favors of Queen Guinevere at the beginning of May. In one version of the story, *Le Chevalier de la Charrette* by Chrétien de Troyes, a contender known as Meleagant engages in combat for the Queen on May 8, in a magic glade where the leaves are always green. In *Le Morte d'Arthur*, Sir Thomas Malory uses a similar name when he has Guinevere abducted by "Mellyagraunce" and his men, while she and her companions, dressed in green and decked with flowers, moss and leaves, are out a-maying.

THE MAY-POLE

Come lasses and lads, get leave of your dads,
And away to the Maypole hie,
For every he has got him a she,
And the fiddler's standing by.
For Willie shall dance with Jane,
And Johnny has got his Joan,
To trip it, trip it, trip it, trip it, trip it up and down.

(TRADITIONAL SONG)

> I have heard it credibly reported (and that *viva voce*) by men of great gravitie and reputation; that of fortie, threescore or a hundred maides going to the wood over night, there have scaresly the third part of them returned home againe undefiled.
>
> (THE ANATOMIE OF ABUSES, PHILIP STUBBES, 1583)

Of all May-Day celebrations, the image of people dancing around a May-pole is probably the one that first springs to most people's minds. As well as the gathering of flowering hawthorn from the woods, it was also the custom to collect a "May-tree" which, usually stripped of its branches, would be set up in the center of the village, decorated with flowers and long ribbons.

The May-pole, representing the Green Man who personified plant life, was a powerful fertility symbol. It both embodied the vegetation spirit and contained his seed. Placed, phallus like, into the womb of the Earth, the seed

Raising the May-pole, in an 1854 engraving by E. Goodall—a joyful occasion attended by all the community, and cause for much merriment.

Crowds gather on the village green to watch the May-pole dancers. Notice the second May-pole in the background.

Bringing Home the May-pole

Against May, Whitsonday, or other time, all the yung men and maides, olde men and wives, run gadding over night to the woods, groves, hils, and mountains, where they spend all the night in plesant pastimes; and in the morning they return, bringing with them birch and branches of trees, to deck their assemblies withall. And no mervaile, for there is a great Lord present amongst them, as superintendent and Lord over their pastimes and sportes, namely, Sathan, prince of hel. But the chiefest jewel they bring from thence is their May-pole, which they bring home with great veneration, as thus. They have twentie or fortie yoke of oxen, every oxe having a sweet nose-gay of flouers placed on the tip of his hornes, and these oxen drawe home this May-pole (this stinkyng ydol, rather), which is covered all over with floueres and hearbs, bound round about with strings, from the top to the bottome, and sometime painted with variable colours, with two or three hundred men, women and children following it with great devotion. And thus beeing reared up, with handkercheefs and flags hovering on the top, they straw the ground rounde about, binde green boughes about it, set up sommer haules, bowers, and arbors hard by it. And then fall they to daunce about it, like as the heathen people did at the dedication of the Idols, whereof this is a perfect pattern, or rather the thing itself.

(*The Anatomie of Abuses*,
Philip Stubbes, 1583)

it held could then be given life, so that all forms of life might flourish. The old European custom of burning a tree in the May bonfire hints at the God's sacrificial death.

To strengthen the May-pole's magic, a group of dancers, holding on to the ribbons attached to the pole, would circle round and round it, binding it with its ribbons. The physical energy of their dancing, the drumming rhythm of their feet vibrating into the Earth, and their circling motion like the motion of the Sun, were all ways of "raising the power," of plugging into the universal force of creation—rather like turning a generator to invoke the mysterious force we call electricity.

DANCING IN THE STREETS

Dance then wherever you may be
I am the Lord of the Dance, said he,
And I'll lead you all, wherever you may be,
And I'll lead you all in the dance, said he.
(SYDNEY CARTER)

Maytime is a time for dancing, if not in the magical circle around the May-pole, then in energy-raising procession through the streets. In these troops of dancers, we see the whole cast of Beltane characters—the May Queen, the Green Man, the Horned Animal God, as well as white Summer and black Winter.

One such dance involved milkmaids leading a flower-garlanded cow, or someone known as a "silver man." He would be a chimney sweep, a figure of blackened Winter, wearing a cage of green branches and leaves hung with silver platter and jugs, and thereby transformed into Jack-in-the-Green, trapped in a cage of green and silver-white Summer. Around these central figures danced the imps of Winter—more chimney sweeps in black suits with blackened faces.

In the Celtic preserve of Cornwall, where many old traditions have been retained, processions of dancers take to the streets on May Day at Padstow in the north, and at Helston in the south on May 8, which is known as Floral

KEEPING UP TRADITION

Despite a temporary setback during the Reformation when Church authorities tried to stamp out the May-Day revels, the people of England hung onto their ancient pagan rites, as described by one observer in 1724:

"There is a May Pole near Horn Castle, Lincolnshire, where probably stood an Hermes in Roman times.

The boys annually keep up the festival of the Floralia on May Day, making a procession to this hill with May gads (as they call them) in their hands. This is a white willow wand, the bark peeled off, tied round with cowslips, a thyrsus of the Bacchanals. At night they have a bonefire, and other merriment, which is really a sacrifice, a religious festival."

[*hermes*, a herm or phallic pillar; *thyrsus*, a wand with pine-cone tip, emblem of the god Dionysus or Bacchus]

In a village in the North of England, jingling Morris dancers in traditional costume keep up a centuries-old custom.

MORRIS DANCERS

Morris dancers may still be found in England on May Day, as they were back in the sixteenth century: "They tie about either leg twenty or forty bells, with rich handkerchiefs in their hands ... borrowed for the most part of their pretty Mopsies and loving Besses, for bussing them in the dark....Then march this heathen company towards the Church and Churchyard, their pipers piping, their drummers thundering, their stumps dancing, their bells jangling, their handkerchiefs swinging about their heads like madmen, their hobby horses and other monsters skirmishing amongst the rout. And in this sort they go to the Church, and into the Church (though the Minister be at prayer or preaching) dancing and swinging their handkerchiefs over their heads like devils incarnate, with such confused noise, that no man can hear his own voice."

(THE ANATOMY OF ABUSES,
PHILIP STUBBES, 1583)

ance Day or "Furry Day." One dancer that did—and does—accompany the others here is the hobby-horse. Originally dressed in a real, black horse skin, he now wears a manmade costume in which he sways about, perhaps demanding kisses or an embrace from the young women, which is curiously reticent behavior for a fertility spirit.

Such quaint customs as dancing through the streets, dressing up as hobby-horses, and circling the May-pole, are quite clearly pagan in origin. What is so extraordinary is the great antiquity of their origins—this is old, old magic. The hobby-horse and the sacred dance to "raise the power" take us on a journey through time, past Christians, past Romans, past Teutons, past Celts, to the far end of the continuum of human perception—the world of our early Stone Age (Paleolithic) ancestors. In cave paintings in France dating from 20,000-8,000 B.C., animal-shamans are depicted, dancing themselves into mystical union with the animal soul of Nature, its knowingness and its power. Although a large proportion of the animals painted on the cave walls are horned (for example, bison and wild ox), as much as one third of them are horses. The imprint of a circle of human feet has also been discovered—feet that perhaps once moved in a magic circle much as May-pole dancers continue to do thousands of years later.

SUMMER'S LEASE

Shall I compare thee to a Summer's day?
Thou art more lovely and more temperate:
Rough winds do shake the darling buds of May,
And summer's lease hath all too short a date...
(*SONNET 18*, WILLIAM SHAKESPEARE)

There are several versions of the trials of the famous lovers of medieval romance, Tristram and Isolt. Unlike the one in which both meet their tragic deaths, in the following version Tristram defeats his rival March when the latter gives the wrong answer to Arthur's challenge—and so wins Isolt, thereby extending, for himself at any rate, summer's lease of love for ever.

So that there might be peace between their countries, King March of Cornwall sent to ask for the hand of Isolt the Fair of Ireland, daughter of King Anguish. The envoy he sent on this errand was his nephew Tristram the Sad, so-called because his mother had died in giving him life. March's offer was accepted, and Tristram set off with Isolt, back across the sea to Cornwall where her bridegroom awaited her.

Before Isolt had left Ireland, she had been entrusted with a magic potion—some say by her mother, some say a wizard—that she was to drink with her new husband on their wedding day. This potion had the power to inspire undying love in the heart of one for another. The voyage was long and the sea was calm, and Tristram and Isolt, sitting on the deck of the ship, felt the need for refreshment. Isolt's maid, Golwg Hafddydd (meaning Aspect of a Summer's Day) went below and, without knowing its contents, her innocent hand grasped the flask that held the magic potion, and it was this that she served. No sooner had a few drops passed the lips of Tristram and Isolt than they looked into each other's eyes—and fell deeply and irrevocably in love.

The path of true love winds a crooked way, and a promise to a king is a promise, so—despite their passion for each other—Isolt was forced to marry March while Tristram tried to relieve his sorrows wandering the wide world. Secret messages and guarded assignations were the only contact the lovers had till, at last, weary of their separation, they eloped to the Forest of Caledon in the north. Here they lay together on a bed of leaves, and fed on the food of love.

Furious at their flight, King March took his grievance to Arthur, High King of Britain, who advised him to send first the finest poets and harpists, and then Gwalchmai, the Hawk of May, to tempt the lovers from their silvan hideaway. Persuaded out of their grove, the pair agreed to Arthur's solution: that Isolt should spend the half year when the trees are in leaf with one man, and the other half, when the trees are bare, with his rival. As the aggrieved party, March was given first choice as to which half-year he would like. Thinking of the longer nights of Winter when he could have Isolt in his bed, he chose the time when the trees are bare. Overjoyed, Isolt burst into song, because March had given the answer had hoped for: there is *never* a time when all the trees are bare—the holly, the ivy, and the yew stay green all year round.

And so Tristram won his Isolt for all time, and the lovers married, and lived in happiness to the end of their days.

Opposite: The May Queen and Lord of the Greenwood: Maid Marian and Robin Hood, surrounded by his Merry Men, carouse in their leafy hideaway.

MAID MARIAN AND ROBIN HOOD

What was he doing, the great god Pan,
Down in the reeds by the river?
Spreading ruin and scattering ban …
(*A MUSICAL INSTRUMENT*, ELIZABETH BARRETT BROWNING, 1806-61)

If any two figures can be said to sum up the spirit of May, it is those of Maid Marian and Robin Hood: in English tradition, May Day was their honorary day. These popular folklore characters are so familiar through countless stories, books, and even films, that we often accept them at face value—but if we bother to look again at what we know so well, we discover something altogether wilder.

Robin and his men dress in green and inhabit the greenwood. As well as his obvious association with verdure, Robin is a rogue, a prankster, an anarchic figure whose center of operations is the forest, an archetypal Otherworld which lies beyond the predictable and the known—all of which gives him a decidedly Pan-ish air. The word "Robin" has various connotations: it is said to be connected with "sheep" and "devil" in French, and was the name for the God of the witches; in Cornwall, it was a term for "penis," and Robin Hood has indeed been depicted as the phallic lord, with ram's horns and legs, leading a coven in their dance. He has also been linked with Merddin, or Merlin, the great wizard of Arthurian legend who, in the forest of Broceliande, transformed himself into such a Shape as eyes had never seen before—the Ward of the Wood, part-animal, part-man—around whom all the wild beasts gathered in such a multitude that none could tell their number.

In the blood of Robin Hood flow two ancestral streams: that of the Green Man, spirit of vegetation, in his leaf-colored costume; and that of the satyr, goat, or stag, the spirit of wild Nature and phallic Horned God known elsewhere as Pan, Dionysus or Cernunnos.

Robin's paramour, Maid Marian, is yet another Maiden and yet another Mary, closely identified with the May Bride of the Saxons and later with the May Queen. She is the White Lady of the woodland who could change

herself into a deer, and who joined her lover and his "coven" for their revels in Sherwood Forest.

The merry pranks of the outlaws fused, in people's minds, with the fun and games of May Day, so that Marian and Robin make regular appearances, as themselves, on this day. The May Queen may be escorted by Robin Hood, and in Cornwall there are traditional mumming plays on May Day in which Robin and his brave band fight on the side of Truth and Justice.

For Robin Hood in particular, May Day was an especially fateful moment for, traditionally, this was the day he died. So while Maid Marian, in true Goddess-fashion, lived on, her lover gave his life to fertilize the land, like many a god-king before him after the sacred marriage ritual with the queen.

THE NIGHT OF WALPURGA

May Eve is the time when German witches celebrated the sacred marriage in an orgiastic festival known as Walpurgisnacht, after the goddess Walpurga, another May Queen. The goddess was later canonized as St. Walpurga and her feast moved to February to avoid any link with May, but the revels continued to be observed on May Eve by witches all over Europe.

The popular view of a witches' sabbath: in this engraving by Jacques Aliament (1726-88), hags perform their dark and secret ritual, attended by their familiars and all the inmates of Hell.

With the aid of her waiting woman, Lady Godiva disrobes in preparation for her ride through the streets of Coventry. A Godiva figure was one of the main participants in old May-Eve processions.

LADY GODIVA

Ride a cock-horse to Banbury Cross,
To see a fine lady upon a white horse;
Rings on her fingers and bells on her toes,
And she shall have music wherever she goes.
(TRADITIONAL NURSERY RHYME)

Another well-known character who is abroad at this time is Lady Godiva. The famous Godiva of legend was said to be the Lady of Leofric, Earl of Mercia and Lord of the town of Coventry. When, in 1040, the Lord imposed heavy taxes on his people, his wife begged him to relent. He offered her a challenge: he would agree to her request if she, in turn, would ride naked through the streets of Coventry. She accepted his challenge, but contrived, popular tradition has it, to cover herself with her hair so that she made her historic ride "neither naked nor clothed."

In old May-Eve pageants, Godiva, symbolizing the shining white Virgin of Spring, appeared with another female figure known as Annis, who represented the black Hag of Winter. (In the "ride a cock-horse" nursery rhyme, Coventry is sometimes substituted for Banbury, and the "lady" is sometimes an old woman with a bonnet of straw, "the strangest old woman that you ever saw.") The name Godiva in fact has Goddess-origins. *Diva* was a universal Indo-European name for Goddess, and *Goda* was an alternative name for the Teutonic love diva, Freya.

THE RIDDLE

The test given to the legendary Godiva was not particularly original—many a divine mistress was presented with a far more difficult task. In Norse mythology, challenged by Ragnar Lodbrog to come to him neither riding nor walking, neither naked nor clothed, neither feasting nor fasting, neither attended nor alone, clever Aslog, daughter of Brynhild, solves her lover's riddle by arriving on the back of a goat trailing one foot on the ground, cloaked in no more than a fishing-net and her hair, an onion to her lips, a hound by her side.

In Celtic lore, Gráinne, the wife of Fionn Mac Cumhaill, leader of the warrior band, the Fianna, falls in love with the hero Dairmaid. She sets a *geasa*—a kind of taboo or magical command—on him to elope with her. Like Lancelot, torn between love for Guinevere and loyalty to Arthur—whose "honour rooted in dishonour stood" and whose "faith unfaithful kept him falsely true"—Diarmaid is caught in an impossible situation. In an attempt to side-step his destiny (and eventual death through Fionn's cunning), he presents Gráinne with a riddle: she should appear to him neither by day nor by night, neither clothed nor unclothed, neither on horseback nor on foot, neither alone nor in company. Gráinne seeks the help of a fairy who provides her with garments made from the "down of the mountainside," which she wears traveling astride a goat in the dusk of the evening.

A riddle with an even darker purpose is found in the ancient British story of Llew Llaw Gyffes. Llew is the unwanted son of the goddess Arianrhod, who lays three curses on him, among them that he shall never marry a mortal woman. The wizard Math circumvents this curse by fashioning for Llew a wife made of the herbs of the hedgerow and the flowers of the forest. She is a Celtic Flora, and her name is Blodeuwedd, which means "flowers." Their marriage is destined to be unhappy, however, for Blodeuwedd falls in love with Gronw, and plots with him to murder her husband. Knowing that Llew's life is protected by enchantment, she elicits from him just how he might be slain—which is neither indoors or outdoors, neither on horseback nor on foot, and only by a spear that has been prepared for a year while the people are in church on Sundays. Gronw at once sets to work on the spear, and a year later, Llew is somehow persuaded to take what must be the most unlikely bath in history. A tub is placed for him by the side of a river, under a thatched shelter, with a goat standing by. While Llew stands perched with one foot on the tub and one on the goat's back, Gronw lets fly his spear. It pierces Llew's side and he takes to the sky as an eagle—returning later to avenge himself.

In all these tales, we see May's favorite theme—romantic love outside marriage—and Godiva's horse (a Celtic symbol of fertility) replaced by the lustful goat.

THE MAY FIRES

As well as the flames of love, real fires played a central part in the festival of Beltane. The kindling of the Beltane bonfire, often on a hilltop where it would be visible for miles, was an important ritual. So that the magic of the flames might not be dissipated, and that they alone might exert their influence over the season to come, all house fires still burning in the area would first be extinguished. Much ceremony then attended the lighting of the bonfire, which had to be kindled in special ways—perhaps by the friction of a fire drill (a twirling stick), by rubbing oak twigs together, or by some method involving the Celts' mystical number, nine.

Druids are said to have chanted spells over the fire, and cattle were driven through it—or between two separate fires lit by Druids—to acquire immunity from disease. In late survivals of the Beltane rites at Dublin, a horse's skull and bones were thrown into the fire, a relic of a more ancient sacrificial victim, whose strength was absorbed by the flames and then transferred to all the animals that passed through them. ("Bonfire" means "fire of bones.") Sometimes the fire might be lit beneath a sacred tree, or a tree or a pole covered with greenery burned in the center, both being symbolic of the sacrificial Green Man and forerunners of the May-pole.

The beneficial power of the Sun was invoked, too, as people danced *deiseil* (sunwise) around the fire, or ran through the fields with burning torches or bunches of straw.

Further vestiges of sacrificial burning are glimpsed in the old Scottish custom of the Beltane cake. This cake, of which one part was blackened, was broken up and shared among the people present. Whoever received the blackened portion was called the Beltane *carline*—the one "devoted" or offered up. A mock attempt was made to throw him into the fire, or he himself had to jump three times through it. The others then referred to him as "dead." This leaping form may have represented Bel or Balder—in country districts of Scandinavia, the May fires are still called "Balder's balefires."

In Scotland, Beltane cakes were also rolled, Sun-like, down a hill, and a cake's breaking at the bottom foretold death for its owner. Alternatively, part of a cake might be thrown over someone's shoulder, with a prayer for the protection of their livestock.

STARTING THE BELTANE FIRE

Nine was a sacred number for the Celts, and one with great potency. As such it was an appropriate number to use in the lighting of magic fires. In Scotland, the Beltane fire was started with nine sticks from nine different trees, gathered by nine men. In Wales, those present must first make sure that they had no iron or metal about their person, such as coins, knives, or buttons (iron, in particular, counters the powers of magic and is much disliked by the fairy folk). Then, as before, nine men must collect nine pieces of different wood, which they should place crosswise inside a circle marked on the ground.

THE WATERS OF MAY

A fair maid who, the first of May
Goes to the fields at break of day
And washes in dew from the hawthorn tree
Will ever after handsome be.
(TRADITIONAL RHYME)

As the year passes through Beltane's gateway, the *uschabheagh*, or the water of life, becomes particularly potent. Washing in May-morning dew is an especially effective beauty treatment, and even more so if the dew used is that found frosting the grass under oak trees, or sparkling on the leaves of the ivy. Anyone who washes in it should make a wish at the same time.

May's magical waters were adopted into Christianity, too. Ascension Day, on May 19, was the day Heaven's clouds parted to receive the risen Lord Jesus. Accordingly, if the skies open again on this day and rain falls, such water from Heaven will have great curative powers, especially for sore eyes.

Early on May morning is also an excellent time to collect the healing waters from sacred wells; Beltane and other days in the month have remained popular occasions, even in fairly modern times, for well-visiting and well-dressing. Like the prancing hobby-horse, the connection of well water with magic is immemorially old—research suggests that some springs have been venerated since the Stone Age.

Ancient or modern, the practice of well worship follows a familiar pattern. The supplicant should, of course, always circle the well *deiseil*, taking care not to utter a word. After praying to the spirit of the well, he or she may then drink or bathe in the water, or use it to wash whichever area of the body is afflicted. One of the most powerful parts of the magic is to offer some item to the divinity—perhaps a piece of cloth or clothing attached to a tree nearby, or a coin or pin, first rubbed onto or pricked into the sore part, and then thrown into the well.

Such offerings may once have served simply to unite the donor with the general beneficence of the well's deity, but they are also expressions of more immediate, contagious magic. These physical objects, having been in such

close bodily contact with the supplicant, contain the very sickness with which he or she is afflicted; offering them to the well is a way of creating a link with the healing spirit that resides in the sacred water—a way of setting up "receivers," as it were, tuned into the curative frequency of the well's "transmitter." Such was the magical charge of these rags, coins, etc., that if anyone stole them they would supposedly catch the disease which these objects contained.

The water in holy wells and sacred springs is a gift from the Earth, and at Beltane its healing powers are magnified. The elaborate cover of this well, known as the Chalice's Well, attests to the importance given it by the local people.

CHAPTER 7

THE GATES OF DAWN
THE OTHERWORLD OF BELTANE

Our revels now are ended. These our actors,
As I foretold you, were all spirits and
Are melted into air, into thin air:
And like the baseless fabric of this vision,
The cloud-capp'd towers, the gorgeous palaces,
The solemn temples, the great globe itself,
Yea, all which it inherit, shall dissolve
And, like this insubstantial pageant faded,
Leave not a rack behind. We are such stuff
As dreams are made on, and our little life
Is rounded with a sleep.

(PROSPERO IN *THE TEMPEST*, ACT 4, SCENE 1, WILLIAM SHAKESPEARE)

J ust as each day has four divisions—noon and midnight, dawn and dusk—so the Celtic year has similar divisions. Because Celtic days ran from evening to evening, Samhain, when the Celtic year begins, equates to dusk when the Moon becomes visible; Beltane, halfway through the year, equates to dawn, when the Moon begins to disappear. By the same analogy, Imbolc and Lughnasadh would represent midnight and midday, respectively the Moon's zenith and nadir.

These thresholds between one period and another are fissures in the wheel of time—gaps in existence when the normal laws that govern human life are suspended, flashbacks to the primordial chaos of the Beginning out of which orderly Creation emerged.

Since Beltane is one of the two main transition points of the Celtic year (Samhain being the other), its gap in time and existence is particularly wide. In the language of

Beltane, and Midsummer later on, are two turns of the year when the fairies are abroad in force. In this relief based on Shakespeare's tale of enchantments, A Midsummer Night's Dream, Titania, Queen of the Fairies, *dallies with the ass-headed mortal, Bottom the weaver.*

THE PEOPLE OF THE HILLS

How beautiful they are,
The lordly ones
Who dwell in the hills,
In the hollow hills.

They have faces like
flowers,
And their breath is wind
That stirs amid grasses
Filled with white clover.

Their limbs are
more white
Than shafts of
moonshine;
They are more fleet
Than the March wind.

They laugh and are glad
And are terrible;
When their lances shake
Every green reed
quivers.

How beautiful they are,
How beautiful
The lordly ones
In the hollow hills.

(THE IMMORTAL HOUR,
FIONA MACLEOD, 1922)

magic, such an interval is known as a "crack between the worlds." It is now that the veil between the Otherworld and the world of man thins to gossamer fineness, allowing a glimpse of—or even access to—the other side. It is now that the unseen becomes the seen, now that all manner of fairy beings pass through the wide-open doorway leading from the land of the spirits into the land of mortals.

STRANGE HAPPENINGS

At such a propitious moment as Beltane, it is only natural that incidents of the greatest curiosity and import should occur. It was on May Eve that the invaders Partholón, the *Tuatha Dé Danann*, and the sons of Mil arrived in Ireland. It was on May Eve that the child Taliesin, mystical bard, emerged from the royal salmon nets in which he was ensnared. It was on May Eve, too, that a terrifying scream could be heard the length and breadth of Britain, that left barren all animals, trees, water and earth. This scream came from a dragon in combat with another, deep in the heart's core of Ireland.

The coming of the Tuatha was of profound importance for they were the gods of the Irish Celts—and forerunners of the fairies. Said to be one in a series of invaders of Ireland, their story and that of the others has been preserved in the medieval *Lebor Gabála Érann*, the Book of Conquests of Ireland—a record in which myth and magic clouds historical accuracy. (A similar, but more fragmented, mythic history of Britain may be traced in the *Mabinogion*, in which the Tuatha are paralleled by the Children of Dôn.)

The first inhabitants, who were largely female, were led by a woman known as Cessair. She and her followers

NOON AND MIDNIGHT

Noon, the Moon's lowest point, is the time when fairy funerals may be seen (whether immortal or not, fairies live a lot longer than humans). It is also a good moment to banish changelings—fairy babies substituted for human ones. Midnight, the Moon's peak moment, is a time for witches—the "witching hour."

perished in the same Flood that Noah survived. The only one remaining was Cessair's consort, Fintan, who stayed on in the form of a salmon, an eagle, or a hawk to observe successive invasions.

Some 268 years after the Flood, Partholón and his people—24 women and 24 men—landed in Ireland, bringing with them domesticated cattle, a knowledge of how to work gold and brew beer, and the first cauldron. They were opposed by a race of demons known as the Fomoire—hideous creatures with single arms and single legs—who used magical weapons against them. Partholón defeated these enemies, but 300 years after their arrival, he and his people were ravaged by plague, and came together to die on the original treeless plain of Ireland.

Next to arrive were the people of "Nemed." When afflicted by the same plague that had decimated Partholón's followers, they were unable to defend themselves against the Fomoire, who rose again. The victors exacted from the vanquished a terrible tribute: every year, on November 1 (Samhain), they had to render two-thirds of their newly born children, two-thirds of their cattle, and two-thirds of their milk. Finally, the remaining survivors of the people of Nemed fled, splitting into three groups. The descendants of two of these groups were later to return to Ireland as the next two waves of invaders.

The first were the Fir Bolg who, with the Fir Gaileoin and the Fir Domnann, arrived on August 1 (Lughnasadh). These were aristocratic, warrior people, and their names suggest a possible connection with Celtic tribes of continental Europe, who were known by the Romans as the *Belgae*, the *Galli*, and the *Dumnonii*.

The Fir Bolg were still in occupation when, on May 1, an event of the greatest significance took place. Dark clouds welled up and filled the sky; settling on a mountain

A distinctively Celtic lattice design, made of a fourfold pattern within the whole of the circle. Such entwining forms suggest the ancient, Stone Age concept of the spiral of life, death, and rebirth. The snake-like heads also imply regeneration, for the snake is born again when it sheds its skin.

top, for three days they blotted out the Sun—these clouds were the celestial chariots of the Tuatha Dé Dannann, the people of the goddess Danu, a race of the greatest beauty and exceeding all others in every art. The Tuatha defeated the Fir Bolg at the first battle of *Mag Tuireadh*, and seven years later confronted the Fomoire at a second battle of the same name. The battle was fought with both sides using weapons of magic, and the Tuatha were victorious.

The last invaders were the Sons of Míl—(or Miledh, a legendary Spanish king whose sons were probably the first Gaelic Celts to invade Ireland, according to myth in about 1,300 B.C.). Having traveled through Egypt, Crete, and Sicily, the Sons of Míl had arrived in Spain, where one of their number had sighted Ireland from the top of a tower. They set sail and their chief bard, Amairgen, announced their footfall on Irish soil with his renowned chant, beginning, "I am the Wind on the Sea, I am the Wave of the Ocean …." After various setbacks and negotiations—including being persuaded to take to sea again (exacerbated by the Tuatha who sang up a wind which had to be stilled by a poem from Amairgen)—the Sons of Míl finally overcame the Tuatha to become rulers of Ireland.

Irish tradition says that the divine Tuatha, dispossessed, took refuge within the hills and ancient burial mounds, to become the *daoine sídhe*, the people of the hills—or just the *sídhe*, dwellers synonymous with their dwellings. They are there still, these "ghosts of the gods" in the abode of the ancestors: they are the beings we call fairies. Some say that they are tall and stately, as befits their divine ancestry; others say that they have gradually shrunk in size, starved of spiritual nourishment by humans who have ceased to revere them, to become the "little people" of legend.

THE FOUR TREASURES

The Tuatha Dé Danann had four magical treasures with which they were able to protect the fortunes of their people. They were the Great Fál, a stone which cried out whenever a lawful king of Ireland sat on it; the spear of the god Lugh, which made its owner invincible; the sword of Nuadu, king of the Tuatha, from which no one could escape when it was drawn from its scabbard; and the cauldron of the Dagda, father of the Tuatha or the "good god," which never emptied and from which no one ever went away unsatisfied.

With these wonders, the Tuatha effectively commanded fate and all the elements, the length and breadth of the world, for they held in their hands the stone of Earth, the spear of Fire, the sword of Air, and the cauldron of Water, which correspond respectively to North, South, East, and West.

The fairies have always been spirits of nature. In this 1925 illustration, Cicely Mary Barker shows one of her diminutive Flower Fairies—the one that inhabits and guards the Stitchwort.

THE LAND OF FAERY

The land of faery
Where nobody gets old and godly and grave,
Where nobody gets old and crafty and wise,
Where nobody gets old and bitter of tongue.....
Land of Heart's Desire,
Where beauty has no ebb, decay no flood,
But joy is wisdom, Time an endless song.
(*THE LAND OF HEART'S DESIRE*, WILLIAM BUTLER YEATS, 1865-1939)

As well as the subterranean Otherworld of the hill, there were also Otherworlds under the sea and across the water—islands towards the setting sun—to which some of the Tuatha fled. All have the features of an ideal world, as in the Elysium of Greek myth: flowery plains and lands flowing with mead and wine, where there is no pain, no aging, nor the other constraints of the physical world, but music, eternal youth, and love free from guilt. Among these paradises are the Irish *Tír na n'Oc*, the Land of Youth; *Mag Mell*, the Field of Happiness; and *Tír fo Thuinn*, the Country-under-Wave, where grow the magic hazelnuts, the kernels of all wisdom. British paradise islands include Avalon— the Island of Apples, likened to the Garden of the Hesperides of Greek legend that lies in the far west, where the apples of immortality grow—the Isle of Joy, and the Land of Women. There is also *Caer Arianrhod*, the shining castle of the goddess Arianrhod, the endlessly circling Silver Wheel of the Stars, the *Corona Borealis* or Crown of the North Wind. It is here that kings, poets and magicians retire until the time comes for them to be reborn. The location of this castle "at the back of the North Wind" is a common Celtic synonym for the Land of the Dead.

These, then, are the visions of fairyland, which find expression in the fairy stories of Celtic as well as other traditions. Entrance to them might be through a mist, or via a form of tunnel, an appropriate mode of entry to a subterranean Otherworld. Jumping or falling down a well—like Lewis Carroll's Alice—or creeping down an underground staircase, visitors find themselves in a Wonderland of flowery meadows or jeweled forests. This mystical method of entry reflects historical fact, for it was normal practice in ancient times to dig pits or shafts in the ground to link the world above with the world below, as a kind of symbolic birth canal to and from the womb of Mother Earth.

A Race in Fairyland, based on an original by Harrison Cady, c. 1903, supports the view of the fairies as the "little folk." Visions of Faerie seem to have had particular fascination for creative minds in the late Victorian and Edwardian ages, producing such classics as Peter Pan and Wendy, *a "Boy's Own" adventure in the Otherworld.*

A magic circle: toadstools mark the place where, by tradition, the fairies are said to dance. Such circles are known as "fairy rings."

ELVES AND FAIRIES

Meddle and mell
Wi' the fien's o' hell,
An' a weirdless wicht ye'll be;
But tak' and len'
Wi' the fairy men,
Ye'll thrive until ye dee.
(TRADITIONAL SCOTTISH RHYME)

The fairy community is aristocratic and hierarchical, having a queen and sometimes an Elfin King, ruling over various classes of fairy. The Fairy Queen of Irish and British tradition is Queen Mab or Medb. Among her court are elfin knights and, further down the social ladder, there is the fairy shoemaker, the leprechaun, *leith bhrogan* or artisan of the brogue. There are also helpful brownies, malicious goblins, and the pooka or boggart—the bogeyman and prototype of Puck in Shakespeare's *A Midsummer Night's Dream*, a kind of Robin Hood—and the *bean sídhe*, the banshee, whose wail can be heard when someone is about to die.

Scandinavia and Germany have similar traditions, the Anglo-Saxon *aelf* giving us the English elf, and linking with the German *elf* and Norse *alf*, while the *trow*—the fairy of the Shetlands and Orkneys—derives from the Norse troll. In Scotland, the elves are divided into two classes: the "gude fairies" or the "Seelie Court" (similar to Germanic *seelig* meaning "holy"), who are helpful to mankind, and the "wicked wichts" or the "Unseelie Court", who plague them with troubles.

The fairies are great lovers of music, song, and dance. Even if the company itself cannot be seen, their music and their singing may sometimes be discerned by human ears. Dancing perhaps in a ring, on a moonlit hilltop, or under the trees, they may try to tempt humans to join them: in Danish and Swedish ballads, a knight by the name of Sir Olave is approached by the Elf-king's daughter, who comes tripping to him from "beneath the greenwood tree" to ask him to lead the dance with her. In some versions, he agrees, although under compulsion; in others, he refuses and dies.

Two other favorite fairy activities are hunting and riding. At times in the year when the worlds open to each other, the fairy court may be heard riding out from the *sídhe*. Mounted on horses with bells a-jingling and elfin horns a-blowing, they proceed on their way in the Fairy Rade—the ride of the fairies.

THE CALL OF FAERY

Come away, O human child!
To the waters and the wild
With a faery, hand in hand,
For the world's more full of weeping
than you can understand.
(*THE STOLEN CHILD*, WILLIAM BUTLER YEATS, 1865-1939)

The traffic between the worlds is not one-way, for at Beltane and other suitable times the fairies might try to spirit humans away with them to their Never-Never Land. When the call comes, some humans go willingly, some unwillingly, and some manage to outwit their temptors.

The Irish hero Connla, for example, is approached by a beautiful woman from *Mag Mell*, the Field of Happiness, who invites him to go with her. She gives him an apple and, while he is considering her offer, the fruit feeds him for a whole month without becoming smaller. When she returns and tells him that the "ever-living ones" request his presence—and that she will take him to a Land of Joy where there are only women—he does not hesitate, despite the spells of a Druid designed to hold him back. He leaps into her crystal boat and sails off with her. Such liaisons are far from uncommon, and perhaps mirror the custom of Irish kings "marrying the land"—the hill-dwelling fairy mistress being the Earth, and her mortal lover representing the community dependent on the Earth.

Babies, of course, have no power over what happens to them, and on May Eve mothers need to be especially watchful for this is when fairies may snatch human infants and substitute changelings of their own. A human woman may then find herself caring for an elfin baby instead of her own. Alternatively, she herself may be whisked off to the Otherworld to act as nurse for the child of the Fairy Queen, and here she will be forced to stay until either released or rescued.

LADY ISABEL AND THE ELF-KNIGHT

Lady Isabel sits in her bower sewing,
Aye as the gowans grow gay—
She heard an elf-knight his
horn blowing,
The first morning in May.

The eponymous Lady of this old ballad manages to resist the charms of the elfin knight by winning a riddling match to retain her freedom, and her maidenhood. On hearing the horn of the elfin knight, she rather foolishly wishes "that horn were in my kist, Yea, and the knight in my arms niest." No sooner said than done, for the elfin knight instantly comes to her bed.

He tells her that if she wants to be married to him, she must make him a "sark without any cut or hem," sewn without needle and thread, washed in a well "where the dew never wat nor the rain never fell," and dried upon a thorn bush that has "never budded sin Adam was born."

Undeterred, the Lady counters him with an even more difficult riddle (the refrain, which consists of the two lines in italics above, comes between each pair of lines):

My father he ask'd me an acre o' land
Between the saut sea and the strand.
And ye maun are it wi' your blawin' horn,
And ye maun sow it wi' pepper corn.
And ye maun harrow it with ae tyne
And ye maun shear it with ae horse bane.
And ye maun stack it in yon mouse-hole,
And ye maun thresh it in yon shoe-sole.
And ye maun winnow it in your loof
And ye maun sack it in your glove.
And ye maun bring it owre the sea,
Fair and clean and dry to me.
And when ye've done an' finish'd your wark,
Come to me, love, an' get your sark.

[*kist*, chest; *niest*, next; *sark*, shirt; *are*, plow; *tyne*, harrow point; *loof*, palm]

IN THE LAND OF DREAMS

All is not gold that glitters.

The fairies are rich beyond the dreams of avarice: they live in palaces and halls of splendor, where they have lavish stores of gold, silver, jewels, and other wondrous treasures—the grave-gold of the ancestral burial places. It must be remembered, however, that the Land of Faerie is not governed by the physical laws of man, and that what may seem real there may not be real to us. This shimmering realm is a place of visions and illusions which can crumble to dust in the harsh light of day. Gifts of fairy gold pressed into the hand of some human visitor may transform, on his return to the world, into mere fistful of withered leaves, while the golden halls of the remembered Otherworld may be revealed as nothing but dark, dank, dripping caves.

Another important difference between the worlds lies in the concept of time. For thousands of years, the fairy folk have known what Albert Einstein only later discovered: time is relative. Beings who are immortal or near-immortal do not measure existence in units of minutes, hours, and days, and many a visitor to the Otherworld has thus been caught unawares. After what seemed a brief stay, they have returned to their own world to discover that they have been away not one or two hours, but one or two hundred years, the life they knew vanished, their friends and family long dead. Worse still, they themselves may die, turning to ashes as did one of the followers of the ancient British god Brân the Blessed on returning to his former homeland, his illusory immortality blown away like thistledown in the blast of the material world.

CHAPTER 8

EYE OF HEAVEN AND HEART OF OAK

JUNE 21: SUMMER SOLSTICE; MIDSUMMER

The night has a thousand eyes,
And the day but one;
Yet the light of the bright world dies
With the dying sun.

(*LIGHT* BY FRANCIS WILLIAM BOURDILLON, 1852-1921)

The Summer Solstice on June 21 is a key date in the solar calendar, for the Sun has reached its highest point in the sky, making this the longest day in the year, and therefore a time for great rejoicing. The solar god is now at the pinnacle of his power, having grown to full maturity: he personifies the Father and the King, who embody the traditionally masculine qualities of strength, energy, and authority. The Goddess, meanwhile, has reached a similar stage in her eternally shifting and returning cycle: she is the Full Moon of Summer in all her glory, the fertile, fulsome Mother Goddess and Queen. This royal pair are perfectly expressed in the symbolism of the Tarot as the Emperor and the Empress.

There is, however, a disheartening side to the celebration. If the Solstice is the day of the Sun's greatest power, it follows that the day after it is the beginning of his gradual decline. In the same way as the Winter Solstice is the "midnight" of the year, marking the moment before the Sun's rebirth, so the Summer Solstice is "midday," marking the start of the Sun's slow decline into night. From now on, the days will slowly but inexorably become shorter as little by little the darkness swallows the light. Thus the Solstice that greets the solar god's zenith is also a good-bye—an *ave atque vale*, a "hail and farewell" to the Eye of Heaven.

The stone circle at Stonehenge, dating from around 1,500 B.C., is all that remains of the third and final temple built on this sacred site. The first was a lunar temple, constructed in about 2,800 B.C. The second was a solar temple, from about 2,400 B.C. The stones are so aligned that sunrise at the Summer Solstice appears directly behind the Hele Stone.

THE MIDSUMMER MOON

June is named after Juno, the Roman Mother Goddess and Queen of Heaven, consort of Jupiter, the Father God (in Greek, the pair were Hera and Zeus). In Anglo-Saxon, June was known as *Aerra Litha*, meaning before Litha, or Midsummer; in Welsh, *Mehefin*, or Midsummer; and in Gaelic, the young month, *An t'Og mhios*.

THE CIRCLE OF STONES

The great Stone Age monument in England known as Stonehenge is one of the most important prehistoric religious sites in the world. Its great stones stand in a circle, the mystical symbol that represents the secret of life—"what goes around, comes around," like the eternally recurring cycles of Moon, Sun, and Earth. The circle and the spiral—endlessly swirling in and out—were the forms chosen for magical dances, and Stonehenge is also known as the Giants' Dance, as if the great standing stones were once superhuman dancers frozen for eternity in mid-step.

The extraordinary effort and skill required to bring the stones to the site, and to construct the monument (between 4,000 and 1,500 B.C.) with limited technology and tools, shows the huge significance it must have had for our ancestors. In this ancient temple open to the sky, the standing stones and the spaces between them are placed with an unerring accuracy that aligns with key points in the Sun's course. At Midsummer, the Sun rises directly behind the Hele Stone, pointing a long, blue finger of shadow into the middle of the circle, like a line on some vast and stupendous sundial.

The Christian temple of Chartres Cathedral in northern France is a storehouse of pagan memories, including this flag stone, placed so that the Sun's rays cast a spot of light onto it at midday on the Summer Solstice.

THE EYE OF HORUS

For the ancient Egyptians, the high-soaring falcon represented the sky itself, in the falcon-headed god Hor, whose watchful eyes were the Sun and the Moon. Hor had many other incarnations. As Horus, he was a sun god, and an eye enclosed within a triangle is an old Egyptian religious motif representing the God entombed in his burial chamber. The fact that the eye is open, not closed, shows that he is not dead but waiting to be reborn. In this phase of his cycle, he stands for his "other half," the Black Sun.

TWIN HALVES

In order to absorb the old pagan festival of the Sun into its own round of holy days, the Christian Church sanctified it with a new name. Just as Christmas on December 25 replaced the birthday of the many pagan Divine Children with the birth of the Christian Sun of Salvation, so June 24—three days after the present Solstice and officially Midsummer Day—was designated the date when St. John the Baptist was born. In this pair of Christian festivals, Christmas and St. John's Day, we see the favorite old pattern of the twins, the two rivals who compete for opposing halves of the year or for possession of a season—like Osiris and his brother Set in ancient Egypt, like the European figures of Black Winter and White Summer who fight it out in mock battle at Beltane, or like the Celtic Tristram who wins from March his beloved Isolt, the spirit of Summer.

Since John the Baptist is deemed to be have been born at Midsummer, the period of time between now and Midwinter belongs to him; on December 25, however, Jesus appears to claim the corresponding period to the next Midsummer. According to tradition, St. John was sent to "prepare the way of the Lord," which he does, relinquishing his authority when his successor arrives like some old pagan father king giving up his throne to his son. Thus the pair continue in an endlessly recurring pattern, going in and out of the alternating doors of the halves of the year, like two figures in a weather clock.

FERTILITY AND FIRE

As sometimes happens, the features of some festivals migrate to another feast later in the year, and some of the traditions of Beltane, the Celtic summer celebration at the beginning of May, spill over to its solar equivalent at the Summer Solstice. As in the former, around June 21 there are fertility rites, fairies, and fortune-telling, morris dancers and "May"-poles—incongruous in this month of June.

Above all, though, the Solstice celebrates the Sun and therefore the main focus now is on the stage he has reached in his annual round. The Green Man honors the grand status of his solar counterpart by showing that he, too, has a more mature side. Although this anarchic figure may still be found, as of old, cavorting with the May Queen at this time of year—in the guise, for example, of Shakespeare's Puck—he also shows himself as the Oak King, the vegetation spirit at his strongest and most regal.

CHARIOT OF FIRE

Fire—mankind's prime symbol of the life-giving Sun—naturally plays a central role at such a significant solar festival. Midsummer is, in fact, the chief fire festival of the solar calendar, and even those who observed the Celtic, lunar-based cycle acknowledged its importance and celebrated it with the sacred flame.

At the Summer Solstice, as the Sun climbs as high in the heavens as he can possibly go, people the length and breadth of Europe from Atlantic shore to old Russia, from cold north to hot south, have lit magical fires in a ceremony of union with the luminous God, in an attempt to boost his power so that he will not disappear too quickly into the depths of winter.

At Midsummer, there were three main ways that fire might be used: huge bonfires might be lit in prominent places; burning torches might be carried in procession around the fields; and flaming wheels might be rolled along the ground or down hills. All these customs are clearly forms of imitative magic. The light of the bonfires, visible for miles, recalled that of the Sun, the torches "blessed" the Earth in the same way as the solar rays, while the spinning wheels mimicked the Sun's rolling passage across the heavens, like the Greek solar god Apollo in his chariot.

One particularly wonderful example of these traditional Midsummer fire rites persisted into relatively modern times in the village of Lower Konz, situated on a hillside overlooking the River Moselle in a wine-growing area of Germany. The basic requirements for the ceremony were a large pile of straw, contributed by each householder in the village, and a huge wheel with an axle projecting about three feet on either side. The wheel was placed at the top of a particularly steep hill, and was wrapped with the straw; any that was left over was made into torches. As the darkness fell, all the men and boys of the community gathered on the hilltop,

Roman observers described the immanitas (inhumanity) of Celtic sacrificial ritual. The victims were often criminals, prisoners of war, or animals. Here, encased in a willow effigy, they wait to be consumed in the Sun god's element—fire. Their number suggests an important, communal ritual.

while the women and girls waited next to a spring halfway down the slope. When all was ready, the mayor of Sierck, a neighboring town, gave the signal and a lighted torch was applied to the great wheel. As this burst into flame—to a great roar from all the people—two young men grabbed the axle handles on either side of the flaming wheel and began to roll it down the slope, Sun-style, towards the river, while the remaining males held aloft burning torches. As the wheel passed the women, they gave a great shout which was echoed by the men still at the summit and by spectators watching from neighboring hillsides.

If the young men managed to plunge the wheel, still burning, into the waters of the Moselle, the villagers of Lower Konz could expect a bumper vintage that year—and a wagonload of white wine in tribute from surrounding villages. Unfortunately, the vines growing on the hillside impeded the wheel's progress so that it had usually burnt out by the time it reached the river. Nevertheless, it was still important for the community to honor the tradition, for without its protective magic their cattle would suffer from convulsions and fits of giddiness, and would take to dancing in their stalls.

Throughout Europe, people trusted their fortunes to the energizing force of the Midsummer blaze. For example, cattle were driven between twin fires to protect them against disease; elsewhere people jumped over the flames, the height of their leap indicating the eventual height of their crops. In France, people believed that the Midsummer fires could banish June rain—as if the flames would call out the Sun who would push aside the dark clouds. In Cornwall, it was thought that if a sufficient number of bonfires could be lit on different hilltops, the landscape would glow with firelight, like a giant reflector dish that would strengthen the Sun.

In Scandinavia, the Midsummer fires were called "Balder's balefires," and were sacred to the god Balder. Naming these fires after the god suggests that his body, in effigy or in the form of a living representative, was once given up in the flames, like some great Viking hero on a sacred funeral pyre.

THE KING OF TREES

In addition to fire, the other key item in the Solstice festival was the oak tree, which provided the most potent fuel for magical fires. In popular imagination to this day, the oak, of all the trees in the wood, symbolizes strength, durability, and longevity. Like proud old men who have survived time and tempest, there are living oak trees still standing after hundreds of years. So evocative are the connotations of this particular tree that it has acquired almost archetypal status in the human psyche. In myth, the oak is equated with, for example, the Greek father god Zeus and his Roman counterpart Jupiter, and with their respective earthly incarnations or semi-divine "sons," Herakles or Hercules, heroes of legendary strength.

The Oak God's special month is June, for in the old Celtic tree calendar the month that ran from June 10 to July 7 was called *Duir*, or Oak. Duir was followed by *Tinne*, the month of the Holly. *Daur*, another spelling of the name, was also an early Irish word for god. Thus, through language, oak, god, and June are for ever linked. For the Druids of Britain and Gaul, the oak was the sacred tree at the center of their cult.

> ### SPIRITS OF THE OAK
>
> The Dryads of Greek myth, like the Celtic Druids, were associated with oak. These female nymphs dwelt within oaks as tree spirits, or outside as their bodily incarnations. The young woman who went by the name of Daphne may have been just such a nymph. Pursued by the god Apollo, she called to her father, a river god, for help, whereupon she was instantly transformed into a tree—thus thwarting the lustful Apollo's plans.

For both the High King of Heaven and the High King of the Wood, the Solstice is a pivotal point, as they stand on the Summit of Time, looking back at the upward path of the past and forward at the downward way of the future. Perched at this post, the Oak God resembles the Roman god Janus who appears at the Winter Solstice, for his other name—Duir—is connected with the word "door" in English and in other European languages, coming from the Sanskrit *dwr*. So, like the two-faced Janus who guards the Gateway of the Year at Midwinter from where he looks both ways, the Oak stands in the Doorway of Midsummer, looking back over his shoulder at his golden road to glory and ahead at his decline to come. The image of the Oak as gatekeeper is reflected in the myth of Hercules, who became the doorkeeper of the gods after his death.

Here again we see the pagan pattern of the alternating pair—Father to Son, Old Time to New Time. Although the Oak God himself may die at Midsummer, the mistletoe which the Druids cut from the tree at this time preserved the oak's potency. The plant could be brought out again at the Winter Solstice, as is the familiar custom, to give the Wheel of Life just the impetus it needs to keep turning.

HOUSES OF OAK

Druids and other priestly figures, such as those of Greek paganism, worshipped not within the manmade confines of buildings, but out-of-doors in sacred groves, among the world of Nature which was the source of the divine. In memory of this custom, Irish churches were once described by the name of *dairthech*, which meant oak house and was an ancient druidic name for the sacred grove. It has also been pointed out that the inner structure of church buildings, with their rows of columns, is not dissimilar to the colonnade of tree trunks of the grove.

The broad-girthed, spreading, and powerful oak has been linked with such father gods as Zeus, and with the strong-man hero Herakles. It was also a sacred tree in the druidic cult.

THE HOLLY KNIGHT AND THE SUN GOD

The rhythms of Nature can often be perceived in the underlying form of Arthurian legends, and the rise and fall of the Sun may be found in stories surrounding Sir Gawain. Although he may be no more than a great hero, Gawain—like Cú Chulainn of Irish lore—exhibits a pattern of behavior one would expect of a sun god. In his battle with Sir Lancelot, his strength increases until noon, but then progressively fades until his defeat at sunset.

In the duels with his other adversary, the Green Knight, we again detect a solar pattern. Sir Gawain and the Green Knight, so the story goes, agree to meet in order to behead each other at alternate "New Years." The Green Knight's weapon is a club made of holly. In the tree calendar, *Tinne* is the Holly month immediately after the Summer Solstice. Holly is also a plant sacred to the Roman god Saturn, who rules the Saturnalia up to the Winter Solstice. At Midwinter, Gawain beheads the Green Knight, and then returns "in a year's time" to be beheaded in his turn; in the legend, however, the Green Knight spares him.

Because of his connection with holly, the Green Knight's "rule" extends from the rise of the holly in July to its "death" at the end of December. Conversely, Sir Gawain's ascendancy runs from the end of December, when he beheads the Knight, to the time when he is due to be beheaded in turn. Thus these "New Years" turn out to be the two solstices—Midwinter when the Sun is born and Gawain defeats the Knight; and Midsummer when the Sun dies and when Gawain is to be killed. In this way, the Green Knight and Gawain share the year from solstice to solstice—as do St. John the Baptist and Jesus.

The other striking feature of this story is that neither opponent appears to stop for a moment to question whether he will be able to fight on, despite losing his head. Like the two halves of the growing and declining Sun, the Light Twin knows that he will always rise again to vanquish the Dark Twin, and vice versa.

THE MISTLETOE RITE

The mistletoe that grew on oak trees was especially revered. Evergreen and therefore never-dying, it represented the God's very life essence, its white berries his magical seed. In a holy ceremony, the Druids cut the mistletoe from the oak—a rite that was effectively a castration of the God, the usual precursor among Indo-European peoples to the sacrifice of the God himself. It is believed that the Druids' most favored time for this rite was Midsummer when the oak flowers and, like the Sun, is at the height of his vigor.

According to Pliny, a Roman observer of the Celts of Gaul (modern France), the ceremony was observed on the sixth night of the Moon's monthly cycle, when white-robed Druids would slice the mistletoe from the oak with a golden sickle, and would then catch it in a white cloth before it had a chance to touch the ground. Two white bulls were then sacrificed to the God, with prayers for abundance and prosperity.

It was crucial to adhere to the details of the rite if the mistletoe—the Druids' "all-heal"—was to retain its extraordinary properties. It should not, of course, be culled in an ordinary way as, for example, with a common knife. The tool used to cut it must be worthy of the sanctity of the task—hence the sickle of gold, the superlative metal. The gold is important, too, because it supplants the iron of which the sickle would normally be made. Iron is traditionally a metal which opposes and curtails supernatural powers and is much disliked by Otherworldly beings: witches and spirits, for example, are said to be repelled by horseshoes or iron axes. Iron used in a magic rite would therefore tend to decrease the power of the ritual rather than intensify it.

The reason why iron is considered so antithetical to the supernatural may go back to prehistoric times, when iron supplanted bronze and stone as the chief material for making tools and weapons. The Ancient Ones—the old deities—who had been alive for many thousands of years were Stone Age beings and so were accustomed to stone implements. As the humans who worshipped them acquired new skills in metal-working, the original stone tools would only have been retained for special, religious purposes, so that stone as a material assumed sacred status and association with magic and the divine. Iron, the new-fangled substance which ousted bronze, would have been even more profane than its predecessor, a view that was probably held right across the Old World. When the biblical King Solomon built his temple, for example, "there was neither hammer, nor axe, nor any tool of iron heard in the house while it was in building."

It might also be supposed that peoples living in the peaceful Stone Age tradition, or working the softer metals, must have been in awe of Iron Age invaders, seeing them as a race of wizards, for could they not smelt, mold, and shape this incredible substance, iron? If they were capable of such a wondrous feat, these were masters of magic and must clearly have power over the supernatural. Stone Age spirits and magical influences would therefore naturally shrink and shrivel at the mere sight of iron, emblem of their new rivals' prowess.

The iron replaced by gold in the mistletoe rite is echoed in the color of the berries themselves, which age to a ripe yellow—for the ancient Greeks, the mistletoe was the Golden Bough. The gold also calls to mind the Sun, while the crescent shape of the sickle evokes the silver Moon. The ceremony was in fact timed to coincide with the first

OPPOSITE: The mistletoe that grew on the oak was regarded as particularly potent. Cutting it from the tree was a sacred druidic rite that was most probably carried out during the period around the Summer Solstice.

phase of the Moon's cycle. Just as the Moon controls the tides and women's menstrual cycle, so, in many cultures, it has been connected with the growth and decay of vegetation. The waxing, moisture-bringing Moon governs the "flow" of plant life, and so is a good time for sowing the seed to make it ripen, swell, and grow (a practice once followed in the Scottish Highlands for example); the drying, waning Moon, on the other hand, governs the "ebb" and so is the preferred time for harvesting the crops, which would be spoiled by excess moisture.

Paradoxically, the mistletoe was culled not with a waning, but a waxing Moon; cutting it during the lunar growth phase would have been a way of trapping its full magical potency before it began to fade.

Catching the mistletoe in a cloth was yet another way of preserving its power. The Druids believed that anything that grew on the oak was sent from heaven, a sign that God had chosen the tree. Allowing the mistletoe to touch the ground would somehow sully it, so ensnaring it in mid-air "between heaven and earth" maintained its sanctity.

Because there is comparatively little written evidence of Celtic belief, and because so much of what we know is gleaned from Roman sources during the time of the Empire, no one can be quite sure of the exact identity of the God-in-the-Oak whom the Druids "castrated" in this ceremony. It seems that he may have been a Celtic Zeus—a father god such as the Irish Dagda, perhaps. The white bulls offered to the God and which, according to sacrificial tradition, would also have been his surrogates, certainly suggest Zeus, who in classical myth assumed the form of a white bull in more than one amorous adventures.

The unleashing of an apocalypse—storm clouds glower, and lightning cracks the sky around the Devil's Tower in Wyoming. According to the Norse epic, this was the way the world ended after the killing of Balder.

BALDER THE BEAUTIFUL

The one story that draws together all the threads of Midsummer—the death of the Sun and the descent into the blackness of Winter, the Twins of Light and Darkness (or the Father Son pair), the Oak King of June and the mistletoe, the great bonfires—is the tale of the death of the Norse god Balder and the terrifying destruction that ensues.

Balder, who is a god of the light, is killed by a mistletoe spear—in Scandinavia a plant traditionally plucked at Midsummer. The hand that wields the spear is that of Höd, a god who may be Balder's brother or, according to some, his father Odin in disguise. Balder's body is consigned to the flames in a Viking funeral—he is laid on a pyre and sent, blazing, out to sea. His murder triggers the Beginning of the End—the "Twilight of the Gods," the *Götterdämmerung*, surely one of the most sweeping of all apocalyptic visions ever to form in the dark dreams of mankind.

This ending, however, turns out to be a beginning: the world renews itself, a new Sun shines in a new sky, and Balder returns from the land of the dead. Although the *Götterdämmerung* is one of the grand epics of myth, it mirrors—on a cosmic scale—the old pagan pattern of the alternating seasons, of life-death-life. Light Life is overcome by Dark Death—a pair so often personified as twin brothers or father and son—but later returns triumphantly at the end of his appointed exile.

The End of Summer

Balder was the son of Odin and Frigg, the Norse King and Queen of Heaven, who lived in the palace of Valhalla. So radiant was Balder's beauty that light shone all around him. He was loved by all the gods, all except one, Loki, who tended in the dark garden of his heart a thriving flower of hatred for the young god.

Balder's days were spent in happiness and harmony until one day—for no reason he knew—his dreams became filled with premonitions of death. On hearing of these omens, Frigg, anxious that no harm should befall her beloved son, went to every creature, every plant, every object in all the world and made them swear not to injure him. And so it was that Balder became invincible—no stick, no stone, no bird nor beast would hurt him, or so it seemed. To amuse themselves, the gods hurled at Balder all manner of weapons, while he, protected by magic, remained unharmed.

Loki, meanwhile, was exercising his mind as to how he might bring about the god's downfall. Disguised as an old woman, he elicited from Frigg that there was one plant whose promise she had not sought. It was too insignificant, the Goddess believed, to be able to do any harm. That plant was the mistletoe. Without saying another word, Loki found the mistletoe, plucked it, and returned to the gods, still at their game. Now there was one of the company, Höd, who had not joined in, for he was blind. With guile and cunning, Loki persuaded Höd to try throwing the mistletoe, saying that he would guide his hand. No sooner had the fatal weapon flown from the blind god's fingers than it pierced Balder's flesh, and he fell down dead.

What a wailing and a weeping then rang through the halls of Valhalla. As the news spread of the god's death, every living thing shed tears of sorrow. The gods gave Balder a hero's farewell. They took his body to the sea, and placed it on his ship, along with his faithful horse. Then, after a blessing from the warrior god Thor, they set the pile alight. As the flaming vessel sailed out across the water, the gods and all those present watched the Light of the World disappear.

While his body burned, Balder's spirit traveled to the land of the dead, ruled by the goddess Hel. A messenger was dispatched to Hel, who agreed to release Balder to the upper world on one condition—that this must be the wish of every living thing in Heaven and on Earth. Among all those whom the messenger approached, there was only one, a giantess, who refused to weep for Balder—this was, of course, Loki in disguise again. And so Balder's sad fate was sealed. As a punishment for his treachery, the gods banished Loki from Heaven, bound in chains, but he escaped, and enlisted as allies the gods' old enemies, the giants and the demons.

This was when the real terror began.

THE BEGINNING OF WINTER

While Balder languished in the wintry land of the dead, storm clouds were gathering around Valhalla, home of the gods, and terrible omens were to be seen.

Out of a dark forest in the east came a wolf whose desire it was to devour the Sun. Season after season the predator stalked its prey until at last it caught up with it. First the Sun's rays disappeared, and then the Sun itself—like a great yellow yolk turned blood-red—slipped into the wolf's ravening maw. The Earth was at once enveloped in darkness, snow and ice; brother took to killing brother; and the giants converged to do battle with the gods.

With a roll of thunder that shook the world and a flash of lightning that cracked the sky in two like a shattered dome of glass, came the fire giants, led by Surt, from the Land of Fire in the south. From the Land of Ice in the north came a ship bearing the dead. On this vessel was Loki and the great wolf Fenrir, whose jaws when open stretched from sky to ground. From the west sailed a phantom ship captained by the giant Hrym, pitching about on the great swell of waves lashed by the sea serpent, Midgard, also on its way to the battle.

As this terrible host stormed towards the field of war over the rainbow bridge that joins Heaven and Earth, the rainbow collapsed and burst into flame. The gods and the giants then joined in a battle of the most savage butchery, at the end of which all the gods were dead, and the Universe began to disintegrate. The stars—like birds too tired to fly—dropped from the sky; the Earth, set alight by the fire giant Surt, became a huge conflagration of flame. At last, as if to put out the blaze, the all-consuming waters rose and submerged all in the silent deep-sea of oblivion.

That was how the world ended.

And this is how the world began.

Slowly, from out of the belly of the Flood, a new Earth was delivered, with mountains and valleys and rivers, with singing birds, grazing animals, and fields of corn sown by no known hand. In this brave new world was a new race of gods, among whom were two old familiar faces—those of Balder and Höd. There were humans, too, ready to repeople the world. While the Apocalypse had raged about them, they had hidden deep in the heart of Yggdrasil, the World Tree that frames the Universe. In this sanctuary they had survived while all else perished, sustained by nothing more than the dew of the morning.

CHAPTER 9

THE SACRIFICIAL GOD

AUGUST 1: LUGHNASADH;
SEPTEMBER 23: AUTUMN EQUINOX

I sometimes think that never blows so red
The Rose as where some buried Caesar bled;
That every Hyacinth the Garden wears
Dropt in its Lap from some once lovely Head.
(*THE RUBÁIYÁT OF OMAR KHAYYÁM*, TRANSLATED EDWARD
FITZGERALD,1859)

Lammas, on August 1 (or August 12 in the Old Style calendar), is a pagan festival that commemorates the start of the harvest, in particular the corn harvest. The gathering of other fruits of the Earth may not start until September, and in cold northern regions, the whole harvest may not be in until the end of October. Lammastide, however, specifically honors the seasonal death of the Corn King, the spirit of the golden fields. The meaning of the festival is reflected in its name, for "Lammas" comes from the Anglo-Saxon *Hlafmas*, or "loaf-mass," in honor of the first bread made from the newly cut corn.

The festival belongs not to the solar calendar but to the lunar-oriented Celtic cycle, in which it is known as *Lughnasadh*, after the Irish god Lugh. It partners Imbolc on February 1 in that both divide the mirror halves of the year—Samhain to Beltane, Beltane to Samhain (Halloween to May Day, and vice versa)—into two, according to the Celtic liking for opposing pairs such as light and dark, Summer and Winter.

Along with the rites and customs directly associated with the harvest, Lammas was also a popular time for visiting sacred wells, accompanied by the usual customs as at Imbolc or Beltane; it also provided a good opportunity for divination.

ABOVE: Corn sheaves, breads, fruits and vegetables celebrate autumnal abundance in a harvest thanksgiving display.

RIGHT: Watched by a nun, monks cut the corn with sickles in this illumination from a French "shepherd's calendar" from about 1495. The roundels on the left show Leo and Virgo, the astrological signs governing August and September respectively.

A 15th-century Italian engraving of Sol, the Sun, the male half of
the divine pair who are both entering their dark phases now.
Below the Sun is the lion of Leo, the sign which he governs.

Luna, the Moon, female partner to Sol.
The Moon governs the sea, and below her
the watery sign which she rules.

A 15th-century Italian engraving of Sol, *the Sun, the male half of the divine pair who are both entering their dark phases now. Below the Sun is the lion of Leo, the sign which he governs.*

Luna, *the Moon, female partner to Sol. The Moon governs the sea, and below her is the crab of Cancer, the watery sign which she rules.*

BROTHER SUN, SISTER MOON

Dry August and warm
Doth harvest no harm.
(FIVE HUNDRED POINTS OF GOOD HUSBANDRY,
THOMAS TUSSER, 16TH CENTURY)

With the beginning of the harvest comes a realization that Summer, the season of the Full Moon, is giving way to Autumn, the season of the Waning Moon; all life, both plant and animal, is slowing drifting towards the sleeptime of Winter, the Dark Moon.

The Waning Moon rules the harvest in two ways: not only does it govern Autumn, when harvesting is done, but it also determines the time of the month when the reaping begins. Traditionally, crops were cut in the waning phase of the Moon for at that point—unlike the "swelling" influence of her earlier, waxing phase—she was thought to have a "drying" effect on plant life, an essential quality for a successful harvest. The face of the Moon that governs this period of decline, when the crops can grow no more, is personified as the withering Crone Goddess, who withdraws the life energy that she originally conferred.

Later on in the harvest season comes a similar turning point for the Sun when he, too, like the Moon, is overtaken by darkness. The Autumn Equinox, which falls on about September 23, is a moment of balance when day and night are of equal length, as at the Spring Equinox earlier in the year. However, at the Autumn Equinox the Sun is weakening, not increasing as in the Spring, and on this day, the solar god is finally overcome as the hours of darkness begin to outnumber the hours of light.

Symbolically, at Lughnasadh and the Autumn Equinox the God goes to the Underworld, whether as the dying Sun taken into the Darkness, or as the Corn King who has been cut down and absorbed, as seed, into the womb of the Earth.

In Irish tradition, the festival of "first fruits" on August 1 is significant for more than one reason. Lughnasadh is said to have been named after the god Lugh because his foster-mother, Tailtiu, died at the beginning of August, and he ordered that the first day of that month should ever after be held sacred in her memory. Accordingly, the Assembly of Tailtiu was convened by the king of Tara, the religious and political center of old Ireland, on 1 August, an important gathering which "all of Ireland" was expected to attend if the well-being of the community was to be assured. Going even further into the mists of mythic Irish history, August 1 was also the day on which the Fir Bolg, a warrior aristocracy, were said to have arrived in Ireland; Tailtiu belonged to the Fir Bolg, conferring on the date a double significance.

In Scots Gaelic, Lughnasadh was known as *Lunasdal* or *Lunasduinn*, while in Manx, spoken on the Isle of Man, it was called *Laa Luanys*. The festival was obviously an important one throughout the Celtic world, for it was also celebrated across the water among continental Celts. Under Roman rule, the population of Gaul—now modern France—gathered together at the beginning of August to honor the god Lugus in the city named after him—*Lugudunum*, the Latin for Lug's town, or Lyons as it is now known. Under Roman influence, this Gallic festival was later dedicated to Augustus, the deified Roman emperor, and in Britain it was similarly transformed, being dubbed *Goel-aoust*, *Gul-austus*, or *Gwyl Awst*.

THE SCALES

The Autumn Equinox, when day balances night, coincides with the world's entry into the astrological sign of Libra, the Scales. A few days later on September 29 (October 10 Old Style), Michaelmas is the Feast St. Michael, who was in charge of the souls of the dead and who weighed their good deeds against their bad in his scales—just as in ancient Egypt the heart of a dead person was weighed in the balance against the feather of Maat, goddess of truth.

AUGUST AND SEPTEMBER

The month of August was named after Augustus, Roman emperor and god. In Welsh the month is *Awst*, in Gaelic *An Lugnasda* (the month of Lughnasadh), and in Anglo-Saxon it was *Weodmonath* (the month of weeds or vegetation). Harvesting continued throughout September, the seventh month of the Roman calendar named after the Latin word for seven, *septem*. In Gaelic the month is known as *An Sultuine* (the month of plenty), in Welsh *Medi* (the month of reaping), and in Anglo-Saxon *Halegmonath* (holy month).

MASTER OF ARTS

Lugh, god of Lughnasadh, was a relative newcomer to the inner circle of divine beings of the Irish pantheon. In an attempt to forge an alliance with the demonic, giant race of Ireland, the Fomoire, the Tuatha Dé Danann, the Irish gods, had agreed to a marriage between Cian, one of their company, to Ethniu, daughter of Balor, Fomoire King of the Isles. The child of this union was Lugh, who in his turn fathered—or was reborn as—the Irish hero Cú Chulainn.

One day, when Nuadu, King of the Tuatha Dé, was entertaining guests at a feast at Tara, a young and handsome warrior approached the gates, gave his name as Lugh, and offered his services as a craftsman. The gatekeeper replied that the Tuatha Dé already had such a person. Lugh then went to list all his other skills—he was a smith, a champion, a harper, a warrior, a poet, a sorceror, a healer, a cupbearer, a metal worker—but each time he was denied entry because, as before, others already filled these posts. Finally, Lugh demanded whether there was any one person within the walls of Tara who could claim mastery of all these arts together. There was none such, of course, and the gates opened to him. He was named Samildánach, "the man of each and every art," was welcomed by Nuadu, and helped the Tuatha Dé to defeat the Fomoire, in the process fulfilling the prophecy that he would kill his own grandfather, Balor.

Balor possessed a terrifying weapon—a single, enormous eye that was never opened except on the field of war, when the lid had to be lifted by the strength of four men. Such was the evil of this eye that it rendered powerless any army that looked at it. At the decisive battle of Mag Tuireadh which Balor attended, Lugh appeared, singing a chant and moving across the ground on one foot with only one eye open. Thus the pair of one-eyed adversaries came face to face. Hearing Lugh's voice, Balor commanded that his eye be opened so that he might gaze upon the puny "babbler." This was done and—like David confronting Goliath—Lugh deftly raised his sling and shot a stone into his enemy's giant eye with such force that the eye was pushed right through Balor's head, redirecting its destructive power at the Fomoire themselves.

The single eyes of Balor and of Lugh suggest that they may have been solar deities, the Sun being the Eye of Heaven, and the defeat of one by the other hints at the replacement of one kind of solar worship by another. Lugh's other name was *Lámfhada*, which means "of the long arm," and he has been likened to the British god Llew Llaw Gyffes, Llew of the Sure Hand, whose title Llew also means light. Like Lugh, Llew had a spear and his sling was the rainbow.

Lugh's mastery of so many different skills make him the ideal Celtic hero. His chosen weapons require much more deft handling than the clumsy, giant club of the other Irish warrior god, the Dagda, and this pair stand in similar relationship to each other as do the Norse gods Odin—one-eyed magician, poet, and warleader with a spear that never missed its mark—and crude Thor flailing about with his battle-hammer. Since gods are so often made in the image of man, these two pairs are perhaps a reflection of a change in human society from that of rude, warring tribes to more aristocratic, settled communities.

BURIED TREASURE

Lugh's presiding over a harvest festival may have something to do with his possible role as solar god—the Sun that has brought the corn to ripeness. However, Lughnasadh is not a solar feast but is held in honor of the fruits of the Earth, and was, it will be remembered, inaugurated in memory of the god's foster mother, Tialtiu, rather than the god himself, which supports the idea that the feast now called Lughnasadh replaced an earlier fertility festival. As a mother, Tialtiu would have represented the Mother Goddess, Mother Earth, the source of all fertility. Chronologically Lugh, being her "son," would appear after his "mother," and he also had a late entry to the ranks of the original Tuatha Dé Danann. These mythic clues suggest that his festival, like the god himself, was a comparative latecomer, a newer version of an older feast once held in honor of an earth goddess from the pre-Celtic period.

Tailtiu's death on this day is, in itself, very significant, for in the seasonal cycle the beginning of the harvest is the time when the Earth ceases to bring forth life, and when her "progeny"—the corn or another crop—is cut down. Right across the old pagan world, this dying of the Earth and the "killing" of vegetation was conveyed in mythic picture language as the seasonal death of a fertility figure or vegetation spirit, who might be either female or male depending on the culture and period of origin of the legend. In classical Greek myth, for example, the spirit was the maiden Kore, daughter of the fertile Mother Goddess, Demeter (whose other name, Ceres, has given us our word cereal), snatched while out picking flowers by the God of the Underworld, Hades; in Sumeria, it was Dumuzi, lover of the goddess Inanna. In British folk tradition, the spirit of the corn (and of malt liquor) was known as John Barleycorn, while in France, Germany, and Slavonic countries, the spirit might take the form of an animal—the Corn Wolf, whose

invisible presence could be detected in the rippling of the corn.

Of course, the deaths of these figures was an occasion for some sadness, but there was hope, too, that the corn or vegetation spirit who died in Autumn would be reborn in Spring, as has always happened since time immemorial in the eternal cycle of departure and return. The ceremonial "killings" of the vegetation spirit, the Sacrificial God, were magical rituals to ensure this return. His death was not just something that happened, but something that had to be made to occur, if life was to go on. The Sacrificial God had to be slain in order to be reborn.

The idea that death is a precondition for life is a concept that every gardener will understand. The plant that has flourished throughout Summer ceases, in Autumn, to grow. Where once new greenery burgeoned and flowers blossomed only old leaves and seedheads are left. As the seedheads ripen, they burst, scattering their contents into the soil. Finally, all apparent signs of life disappear. When Spring comes around, new shoots miraculously appear, growing from the seeds of last year's plant and nourished by its remains, the decayed vegetation that has enriched the soil.

This pattern of death giving birth to life is one that recurs every year, but the question is: is the plant that grows in Spring the *child* of the parent plant, or the *parent* reborn? It is effectively both, and here we find the mystery that underlies the great myth of many ancient pagan religions, that of the Goddess and her son-lover who dies and is reborn. The Goddess is the Source from which life emanates, the fundamental Earth, the Mother, the Whole that encompasses both beginning and ending. Counter-balancing to her Whole, there is the Part—her son-lover. The Goddess gives birth to a son (the Earth brings forth the Plant); he becomes her lover and later dies (the Plant withers, having dropped its seed into the Earth); she then gives birth to her lover's son (the Earth brings forth a new Plant from the seed of the old). So, like a plant that is both new and reborn old, the dead and risen God is simultaneously the Goddess's lover and her son.

Some examples of this divine pair are Greek Aphrodite and her lover Adonis; Babylonian Ishtar and Tammuz; and Egyptian Isis and Osiris. The death of the Sacrificial God is always violent, and is bewailed by his mistress. Her grief later turns to joy, however, when her life-bringing lover returns, as he always does.

BLOOD AND BONES

The symbolic spilling of the God's blood (or the actual spilling if the sacrifice involved a real-life surrogate) is part of the fertilizing process—an idea that does not seem so strange when one thinks of the dried blood and bones gardeners use to enrich the soil. In one legend, flowers sprang up where Adonis bled and, in both myth and wonder tale, bones have brought forth new life. In the Greek Flood story, for example, Deucalion and Pyrrha, who had floated in an ark for nine nights and nine days and were the only humans to survive the Deluge, wished to repeople the world. They prayed to the goddess Themis who told them to throw the bones of their "first ancestor" behind them. Puzzled at first, the couple at last understood the divine command: their first ancestor was, of course, the goddess Gaia, their Mother—the Earth herself— and her "bones" were the rocks and stones. The stones that Deucalion threw over his shoulder became men, those that Pyrrha threw became women, and in this way the world was repopulated.

In this modern illustration by Jennie Harbour, Cinderella flees from the ball. There are literally hundreds of variations on the Cinderella theme. Many feature regeneration in the form of a plant or a tree, and all end with transformation and salvation.

In various tellings of the Cinderella story (other than the well-known French version, a literary confection pieced together for aristocratic palates in 1697 by the author Charles Perrault), there is the poignant image of a tree or perhaps a flower growing from the grave that contains the body or bones of Cinderella's mother or some other helper figure. The tree often appears after the hapless girl has watered the grave with her tears, and in its branches a bird, or pair of birds, may sit. This life-from-death motif arises from the same fundamental concept that underlies the myth of the slain and risen God: the tears represent the healing Water of Life, the tree is an archetypal symbol of renewal—the Tree of Life—while the bird, winged creature of the airy heavens, is an emblem of the soaring spirit of life itself. In the Grimm Brothers' tale *Ashchenputtel*, the tree that grows on the mother's grave is a hazel. In *The Juniper Tree* from the same authors, it is the bones of the murdered boy hero that are lain beneath the tree, where his own mother lies buried. With a quivering of its branches and a puff of mist, the tree immediately brings the boy back to life in the form a firebird, whose song reveals the identity of his murderess, the stepmother. After he has avenged himself by killing her in turn, he resumes his former human shape, and he, his father and stepsister "live happily ever after"—precisely the image of resurrection and salvation hoped for in the cutting down of the God-in-the-Corn.

MOTHER AND CHILD

In European folk tradition, as the harvest neared its end the attention of the reapers became focused on the last portion of the crop still standing, for this was redolent with magic: it was where the Corn Spirit had taken refuge. Thus the last sheaf to be cut was often shaped into the form of a human figure, dressed in clothes and adorned with ribbons.

Depending on the view of the particular community, the Spirit-in-the-Sheaf might be seen as old or young. If "old," it was in the sense of "ripe" and "mature," and then the figure made from the last sheaf might be called the Corn Mother, Harvest Mother, Great Mother, Grandmother, *Cailleach* (Gaelic for old wife), *Wrach* (hag in Welsh), *Baba* or *Boba* (old woman in Slavonic languages), or even the Old Man. If "young," the corn figure was seen as the child that has been delivered from its mother when the sickles cut its cornstalk "umbilical cord." In this case, the figure might be called the Maiden, the Corn-maiden, the *Maidhdeanbuain* (shorn maiden in Gaelic), or the Kirn-baby or Kirn-doll, after *kirn* which means corn in Scots and northern English dialect. In Germany the birth of the corn baby was even enacted with fake labor cries, new-born wailing, and all. The part of the mother was played by the woman who had bound the last sheaf, while her "baby" was a boy inside a figure made from the sheaf. This folk custom recalls the rite of the Greek god Dionysus in his role as Corn God, the infant *Dionysus Liknites* symbolically carried in procession in a winnowing basket, for the

Harvest festival celebrations are one of many examples of pagan traditions adopted by the Christian church.

adoration of the worshipping crowd. In the Corn Mother and the Corn Maiden, we also glimpse the images of Demeter and Kore.

The figure formed from the last sheaf played a central part in the joyful processions, dances and suppers of Harvest Home, and was closely associated with the person who had cut, bound, or threshed the corn from which it was made. This person was sometimes given the same name as the figure—for example, the "Old Woman"—and it was often necessary for there to be a link in age, too: when the sheaf was called the Mother, it was the oldest married woman who had to shape it into human form; when called the Maiden, the sheaf had to be cut by the youngest girl. Thus, like the corn figure, the person most intimately involved with it was also seen as a representative of the Corn Spirit.

The last sheaf and the "corn dolly"—as this traditional effigy is now best known—had a magical, fertilizing influence that was put to use in various ways. Some of the grain from the sheaf might, for example, be mixed with the seed corn, or scattered among the young corn in the following spring. The doll itself might be kept in the farmhouse and then broken up and shared among the cattle at Yule to make them thrive in the year to come, or given to the first mare in foal. A Mother sheaf, shaped like a pregnant woman, might even be presented to the farmer's wife to make her fertile and give her a child the following year.

John Barleycorn

Barley is one of the oldest, if not the oldest of cereals cultivated by ancient European peoples. In the following traditional British song, we see the whole life cycle of John Barleycorn, personification of the grain—and his eventual happy end as "whisky." The word is derived from *usquebaugh*, meaning "water of life" in Gaelic (rather like the French *eau de vie*—brandy—product of the fruit of the vine).

There came three men from out of the west,
Their fortunes for to try,
As they had sworn a solemn oath,
John Barleycorn should die.
They ploughed, they sowed, they harrowed him in,
Throwed clods upon his head,
And these three men made a solemn vow,
John Barleycorn was dead.

Then they let him lie for a very long time
Till the rain from heaven did fall,
Then little Sir John sprung up his head,
And soon amazed them all.
They let him stand till midsummer
Till he looked both pale and wan,
And little Sir John he growed a long beard
And so became a man.

They hired men with the scythes so sharp
To cut him off at the knee.
They rolled him and tied him by the waist,
And served him most barbarously.

They hired men with pitchforks
Who pricked him to the heart,
And the loader he served him worse than that,
For he bound him to the cart.

They wheeled him round and round the field
Till they came unto a barn,
And there they made a solemn mow
Of poor John Barleycorn.
They hired men with crab-tree sticks
To cut him skin from bone,
And the miller he served him worse than that,
For he ground him between two stones.

Here's little Sir John in a nut-brown bowl,
And brandy in a glass;
And little Sir John in the nut-brown bowl
Proved the stronger man at last.
And the huntsman he can't hunt the fox,
Nor so loudly blow his horn,
And the tinker he can't mend kettles or pots
Without a little of Barleycorn.

THE DEATH OF TAMMUZ

It was in the month that bears his name, in the burning days of
late summer, that Tammuz—the golden one, beloved of the
goddess Ishtar—was cut down. Cruelly slain was Tammuz—
hacked with sickles, his flesh scattered over the land until it ran
red with his blood, his bones ground, like corn, to flour and
thrown to the winds. When the goddess learned of the death of
her beloved, she bewailed her loss to the heavens:

At his vanishing away she lifts up a lament,
"Oh my child!" at his vanishing away she lifts up a lament;
"My Damu!" at his vanishing away she lifts up a lament.
"My enchanter and priest!" at his vanishing away she lifts
up a lament,
At the shining cedar, rooted in a spacious place,
In Eanna, above and below, she lifts up a lament.
Like the lament that a house lifts up for its master, lifts she
up a lament,
Like the lament that a city lifts up for its lord, lifts she up a
lament.
Her lament is the lament for a herb that grows not in the bed,
Her lament is the lament for the corn that grows not in the ear.
Her chamber is a possession that brings not forth a possession,
A weary woman, a weary child, forspent.
Her lament is for a great river, where no willows grow,
Her lament is for a field, where corn and herbs grow not.
Her lament is for a pool, where fishes grow not.
Her lament is for a thicket of reeds, where no reeds grow.
Her lament is for woods, where tamarisks grow not.
Her lament is for a wilderness where no cypresses grow.
Her lament is for the depth of a garden of trees, where honey
and wine grow not.
Her lament is for meadows, where no plants grow.
Her lament is for a palace, where length of life grows not.

Languishing in her sorrow, the goddess resolved to find her lost
lover, no matter what perils lay ahead. She set off to the abode
where he now dwelt, the House of Darkness, where dust lies on
door and bolt, and from which there is no returning. Here live the
edimmu, the souls of the dead, both the mighty and the humble,
clad, like birds, in garments of wings. Dusk is their only light,
mud their only food.

As Ishtar passed through each of the seven gates of Hell, she
removed one garment or one adornment—the crown from her
head, the pendants from her ears, the necklace from her throat,
the jewels from her breast, the girdle from her waist, the
bracelets and anklets from her wrists and feet, and, last, the gown
that covered her. Thus, naked, she came before her sister,
Erishkigal, Queen of the Underworld. But the Dark Queen
looked with hatred on the Queen of Love, and refused to help
her. Instead, she kept her a prisoner in her palace, and unleashed
on her the Sixty Maladies.

On Earth and in Heaven, all mourned the loss of Ishtar, and all
languished in sorrow, for without Love, nothing can thrive. The
bull refused to cover the cow, the ass no longer approached the
she-ass, and, in the street, the man no longer hailed the maid-
servant. Such was the sorrowing and desolation that at last Sîn,
the Moon, and Shamash, the Sun, appealed to Ea, Lord of Magic,
Master of the waters that nourish the Earth and contain all
wisdom. And Ea created a messenger, Asushu-Namir, and sent
him to the Land of No Return with magic words to overcome the
will of Erishkigal. And even though her own powers were great,
and she tried to bind the messenger with a great enchantment,
Erishkigal could not resist the magic of Ea and was forced
to set Ishtar free.

Thus it was that Ishtar was sprinkled with the Water of Life, and
that she brought her lover forth from the Underworld. But, it was
agreed, Tammuz might spend only half the year in freedom; the
remaining half he must return to be Erishkigal's prisoner.

And so it came to be that, when Tammuz was above the Earth,
Ishtar rejoiced and nature and man flourished. But when he had
to return to the land below, Ishtar grieved and life died. And each
time, unfailingly, the bereaved goddess again made the perilous
journey to the Underworld to bring Tammuz back.

Thus it has been from the beginning of time, and
thus it will be to the end.

(This winter creation myth comes from the Sumero-Babylonian
culture that flourished from 3,000 B.C. around the Tigris and
Euphrates rivers. The month of Tammuz, in which the goddess's
lover was slain, was July, harvest-time in these hot countries. In
the harvest rites, the lament below was sung, with wailing flutes,
over an effigy of the dead god.)

THE HARVEST LOAF

I went sunwise round my dwelling
In the name of Mother Mary
Who promised to preserve me
Who did protect me
Who will preserve me
In peace, in flocks, in righteousness of heart.
(*CARMINA GADELICA*, COMPILED AND TRANSLATED
BY ALEXANDER CARMICHAEL)

The day on which the Virgin Mary was received into Heaven is celebrated on August 15, and is known as The Feast of the Assumption. Christian and pagan traditions came together in a Scottish custom on this day which involved a special harvest loaf, known as *Moilean Moire*, or Mary's Bannock (bannock is a type of bun)—and a wealth of magical detail. Anyone wishing to make this loaf should follow these instructions:

—To make the flour for the bannock, pick new corn, dry it in the sun, husk it by hand, and grind it with stones.

—Kindle a fire with magical rowan-wood, and while this is warming up, make your dough from the flour.

—Knead the dough on a sheepskin, shape it into a loaf, and cook it over the fire.

—When the *Moilean Moire* is cooked, each member of the family, in order of age, should eat a piece, and then all walk *deiseil*, sunwise, around the fire.

—Finally, place the embers of the fire in a pot, and circle with it deiseil around the fields to bless them.

PICKING FRUIT

Later on in the harvest season, fruit will be ready to pick, but the timing of this operation must, as always, coincide with the appropriate phases of the Moon, Mistress of growth and decay. Late fruits should not be gathered until after Michaelmas Day:
The moon in the wane, gather fruit for to last But winter fruit gather, when Michael is past …

(*FIVE HUNDRED POINTS OF GOOD HUSBANDRY*, THOMAS TUSSER)

GIVING THANKS

Although it is not celebrated until late in November in the United States and in October in Canada, the great feast of Thanksgiving is not a Winter festival but belongs to the round of Harvest Home celebrations of the previous season, Autumn. Its specific origins lie not in religious observance but in history for it commemorates an historical event, namely the first harvest of the Pilgrim settlers in Massachusetts in 1621. Threatened by starvation, the settlers had been saved by Native Americans who had shown them how to

Mother Mary is received into Heaven in Titian's The Assumption of the Virgin, *1516-18. The Assumption was not officially recognized until 1950 when Pope Pius XII, petitioned by 8 million Catholics, declared that the people's Goddess had entered Heaven "body and soul."*

THE DEVIL'S WORK

In Britain, Holy Cross or Holy Rood Day—September 14—is traditionally also known as the Devil's Nutting Day, and marks the beginning of the nutting season. Double hazelnuts, growing two to a stalk, picked on this day have the power to banish rheumatism, toothache, and the effects of spells. One should not be too hasty to gather the magic nuts, however, for unripe hazels are extremely unlucky.

In the Old Style calender, Holy Rood Day fell on September 26. During the intervening twelve days between the New and Old Style dates, the Devil's temper obviously sours considerably, for he replaces the lucky hazels of September 14 with the positively inedible blackberries of September 26. According to Scottish tradition, this is the day when the Devil poisons the berries by spitting or urinating on them. In England, the event happens a little later for the Devil needs time to travel south, and does not reach English bramble bushes until Michaelmas on September 29 (or even, if he is especially tardy, Old-Style Michaelmas on October 10).

grow the alien food crops of this unfamiliar land. In a beautiful spirit of true community, newcomers and native people came together to celebrate their first harvest. As Edward Winslow, one of the Mayflower travelers, observed, "Our harvest being gotten in, our governor sent four men on fowling, so that we might, after a special manner, rejoice together after we had gathered the fruit of our labors." The occasion was not nationally observed, however, until after the American Civil War.

HARVEST CHEER

In harvest time, harvest folk, servants and all
Should make, all together, good cheer in thy hall
Once ended thy harvest, let none be beguiled
Please such as did help thee, man, woman and child.

(*Five Hundred Points of Good Husbandry*,
Thomas Tusser)

Nuts of all kinds are the product of the late harvest,
traditionally beginning in September and sometimes
continuing until as late as Halloween.

CHAPTER 10

THE HAG OF NIGHT
OCTOBER 31: SAMHAIN

There was a Door to which I found no Key:
There was a Veil past which I could not see:
Some little Talk awhile of Me and Thee
There seem'd—and then no more of Thee and Me.

(*THE RUBÁIYÁT OF OMAR KHAYYÁM,*
TRANSLATED EDWARD FITZGERALD, 1859)

O n October 31, the world as we know it changes for a brief span. Time, the fourth dimension, ceases to exist, and a doorway opens into a fifth dimension normally inaccessible to man—the space that is the Otherworld.

This last day of October is a major "crack between the worlds," for it marks the end of the Celtic Old Year and the beginning of the New. As Time crosses the threshold between one year and another, it belongs to neither but stands in some space outside itself, beyond the confines of normal reality—and it is then that humankind has a peephole into eternity, and comes face to face with the cosmic realities, with life and death, with Fate.

At Samhain, on October 31, mortals may see the fairy *sídhe*, those beings that dwell in the parallel universe of the supernatural—as they may also do at Beltane, Samhain's summertime counterpart. On November Eve, however, they may have visitors of another kind as well. While Beltane is a time of opening up, Samhain is a time of closing in, when the Earth takes back into herself what she has given. Consequently, it is a time to reflect on the journey of death and to remember those that have made the journey. It is only natural therefore that the dead should choose Samhain as the crack through which to return to visit the living, from their dwelling place within the Earth.

In Mexico, the dead are especially well honored. At midnight on November 1, the Festival of the Dead begins, when lovingly prepared model skeletons representing Death may be seen everywhere.

Samhain is the start of
Winter, ruled by the Goddess
in her Hag persona. Here the
Hag appears in triplicate as
the Graeae of Greek myth,
with the hero Perseus.
Individually, the Graeae
were Enyo, Pemphredo, and
Deino (Warlike One, Wasp,
and Terror). Sharing one eye
and one tooth, they were a
manifestation of the
"three-in-one."

THE DARK NIGHT OF THE YEAR

Naked came I out of my mother's womb,
and naked shall I return thither ...
(*JOB*, CHAPTER 1, VERSE 21)

As well as being a passageway for the dead, Samhain also begins *Geimredh*, the dark, Winter half of the year. This gives credence to its being the Celtic New Year, for the Celts—as Julius Caesar observed—were a "people of the night" whose days began at dusk. By analogy with the Celtic day, Samhain—which ushers in the "night" of the year—may be said to be its dusk or twilight, when the power of the Moon is in the ascendant.

In the lunar calendar, Winter corresponds to the Dark Moon, the three days in each month when the Moon disappears from view. Presiding over this lunar season is the Goddess in the last of her three personae, that of the Hag or Crone who destroys what she has created, taking it back into the black depths of her Earthly womb— "earth to earth, ashes to ashes, dust to dust...."

PASSING THROUGH DEATH

... in another place, the spirit animates the members.
Death, if your lore be true, is but the center of a long life.
("ON THE TEACHINGS OF THE DRUIDS," FROM THE *PHARSALIA* BY LUCAN
[MARCUS ANNAEUS LUCANUS], A.D. 39-65)

Although Samhain is a time of death, for the Celts death was not the specter from which modern humans shrink, a once-and-for-all condemnation to eternal oblivion. Rather, it was one stage in the life-death-life process, a bridge from one existence to another. So strongly did they trust in personal immortality that Celtic warriors were not afraid to die in battle.

Because of the lack of written evidence on the Celtic belief system, we have to rely partly on the observations of the Romans who ruled the Celts of Gaul. According to Julius Caesar, the Druids taught a doctrine of transmigration—that souls did not die but, after physical death, passed into other bodies. Some classical writers, in an attempt

THE DARK MONTH

Samhain ushered in November, known in Gaelic as *An t-Samhuinn*, meaning the month of Samhain; in Welsh, it was *Y Mis Du*, or the black month. The Welsh also knew it as *Tachweld*, the month of slaughtering, and the Anglo-Saxons as *Blotmonath*, the month of blood, for this was the time when animals that could not be overwintered had to be killed.

All the gods of this world were worshipped on this day, from sunrise to sunset.
(TRADITIONAL IRISH SAYING)

to understand this concept, interpreted it according to the model they knew best, that of the philosopher Pythagoras, who maintained that souls passed from one body to another, in order progressively to expiate their sins with each new life until they were finally pure.

However, the Celts had no punitive Hell, no afterlife of reparation, so a concept of transmigration with moral accountability would seem to be foreign to them. It may simply be that the soul of the ordinary Celt—once through the tunnel of death—reanimated the body on the Other Side (as Lucan's observation above implies). The "dead" Celt, then, would not just be a shadow of his or her former self inhabiting a gloomy and punitive Afterworld, but the same person he or she had been in "life," with a new physical body or perhaps even the old body revivified, living in a happy land of immortality.

Such a belief in physical immortality is attested by the profusion of grave-goods (armor, weapons, utensils, ornaments, coins, even chariots) and by the sacrifice and

In this 16th-century print, a winged, skeletal Death bearing an hourglass, with scythes at the ready, rides into war. For the Celtic warrior, death it seems did not mean destruction, but rather transition.

burial of close family members and slaves along with the body, so that the dead person had all that was necessary to resume the old life in the new. Further evidence of this belief is the custom of throwing letters into the grave for the deceased to read once arrived on the Other Side—and for the belief that debts incurred in this life would be repaid in the next.

In our modern world, we do not expect to be visited at Halloween by the living dead, but rather by their ghosts and phantoms—but then we are at the other end of two thousand years of Christian influence, which teaches that the flesh corrupts and decays, and only the soul is immortal.

> ### PHANTOMS ON THE WIND
>
> At dusk on Halloween, the *Sluah*, the Host of the Dead, are said to go drifting by on the wind.

WELCOMING THE DEAD

"How many miles to Babylon?"—
"Threescore miles and ten."
"Can I get there by candle-light?"—
"Yes and back again!"
(TRADITIONAL NURSERY RHYME)

At this, their special festival of remembrance, the dead make their way back from the grave to revisit their old homes. The journey is a long one, however, and the travelers may need help along the way. Accordingly, in Ireland, it was the custom at Samhain to leave the entrances to the burial mounds open, and to light the interiors until cockcrow the following morning so that the dead might more easily find their way along the dark path from the tomb. (In the ancient Egyptian festival of the dead, which occurred earlier in the year, houses were similarly lit to illuminate the way.)

Once the travelers have arrived at their destination, it is only common courtesy to welcome and refresh them with food and drink, as one would any visitor. Accordingly, on All Souls' Eve, the night of November 1, or on the morning of the following day, it was the custom in parts of Europe to bake "soul cakes" or "soul bread" of which the returning souls could partake. In Wales, special food called *bwyd cennad y meirw* was left outside, and, before everyone went to bed, the hearth was carefully prepared for the arrival of the dead relatives.

THE WIFE OF USHER'S WELL

In this old ballad, three sons who had drowned return to see their
mother on Martinmas Eve, November 10, which is Halloween Old
Style, in "earthly flesh and blood"; when the cock crows on
Martinmas morning, however, they must return whence they came.

There lived a wife at Usher's Well,
And a wealthy wife was she;
She had three stout and stalwart sons,
And sent them o'er the sea.

They hadna been a week from her,
A week but barely ane,
When word came to the carline wife,
That her three sons were gane.

Thay hadna been a week from her,
A week but barely three,
When word came to the carline wife,
That her sons she'd never see.

"I wish the wind may never cease,
Nor fashes in the flood,
Till my three sons come hame to me,
In earthly flesh and blood."

It fell about the Martinmas,
Whan nights are lang and mirk,
The carline wife's three sons came hame,
And their hats were o' the birk.

It neither grew in syke nor ditch,
Nor yet in only sheugh,

But at the gates o' Paradise,
That birk grew fair eneugh.

"Blow up the fire, my maidens!
Bring water from the well!
For a' my house shall feast this night,
Since my three sons are well."

And she has made to them a bed,
She's made it large and wide;
And she's ta'en her mantle her about,
Sat down at the bedside.

Up then crew the red, red cock,
And up and crew the gray;
The eldest to the youngest said,
"'Tis time we were away."

The cock he hadna craw'd but once,
And clapp'd his wings at a',
When the youngest to the eldest said,
"Brother, we must awa'.

"The cock doth craw, the day doth daw,
The channerin' worm doth chide;
Gin we be missed out o' our place,
A sair pain we maun bide.

"Fare ye weel, my mother dear!
Fareweel to barn and byre,
And fare ye weel, the bonny lass,
That kindles my mother's fire."

[*carline*, old woman; *fashes*, troubles; *birk*, birch; *syke*, marshy
hollow; *sheugh*, ditch; *chinnerin'*, fretting]

AT THE CROSSROADS

At Samhain the Earth gives up its dead, who come back willingly to visit the living; there are those who are not dead, however, but are prisoners of the Otherworld, and need to be snatched back if they are not to be lost for ever to the world of man. The prisoners needing rescue are humans who have been stolen by the fairies; the ideal time to effect such a rescue is "at the mirk and midnight hour" on the night of Halloween when the years meet, and when the fairies troop out in their jingling, jangling ride; the ideal place is at a crossroads.

The old British border ballad of Tam Lin tells of just such a rescue. This is the story of brave Janet (Jenny) and her lover, who was stolen by the fairies when out riding with his grandfather, and now haunts Carterhaugh Wood as an "elfin knight." Janet goes to the well in the wood, and summons her lover, as one does a spirit, by breaking the branch of a tree sacred to him, in this case a rose. Tam Lin tells her how to free him from the spell that binds him before he—"sae fair and fu' o' flesh"—is offered up as the fairies' seven-year tribute to the Devil. Such a fate will naturally occur at Samhain, when the seventh year ends. Accordingly, she must wait for him on that night at Miles Cross and, as the clock strikes midnight, she will "hear the bridles ring" and will see him come by in the Fairy Rade. Without delaying an instant, she must grab him and fearlessly hold him fast, no matter how much he is forced to shape-shift. If she can maintain her hold until cockcrow when all supernatural forces must vanish, the fairies' power over him will be broken. Jenny follows his instructions to the letter, and so saves her lover.

THE SIN-EATER

To release a soul from its sins so that it would not walk again at Hallowtide, a "sin eater" might be employed:

In the County of Hereford was an old Custom at Funerals, to hire poor people, who were to take upon them all the Sins of the party deceased. One of them I remember (he was a long, lean, lamentable poor rascal). The manner was that when a Corpse was brought out of the house and laid on the Bier; a Loaf of bread was brought out and delivered to the Sin-eater over the corps, as also a Mazer-bowl full of beer, which he was to drink up, and sixpence in money, in consideration whereof he took upon him all the Sins of the Defunct, and freed him (or her) from Walking after they were dead.

(*REMAINS OF GENTILSIM*, JOHN AUBREY, 1688)

The Ballad of Tam Lin

This excerpt from the ballad tells what Jenny has to go through to rescue Tam Lin from the fairies:

"And ance it fell upon a day,
A cauld day and a snell,
When we were frae the hunting come
That frae my horse I fell;
The Queen o' Fairies she caught me,
In yon green hill to dwell.

"And pleasant is the fairy land,
But, an eerie tale to tell,
Ay at the end of seven years
We pay a tiend to hell;
I am sae fair and fu' o' flesh,
I'm feared it be myself.

"But the night is Halloween, lady,
The morn is Hallowday;
Then win me, win me, an ye will,
For weel I wat ye may.

"Just at the mirk and midnight hour
The fairy folk will ride,
And they that wad their true-love win,
At Miles Cross they maun bide."

"But how shall I thee ken, Tam Lin,
Or how my true-love know,
Amang sae mony unco' knights
The like I never saw?"

"O first let pass the black, lady,
And syne let pass the brown,
But quickly run to the milk-white steed,
Pu' ye his rider down.

"For I'll ride on the milk-white steed,
And ay nearest the town;
Because I was an earthly knight
They gie me that renown.

"My right hand will be glov'd, lady,
My left hand will be bare,
Cock't up shall my bonnet be,
And kaim'd down shall my hair,
And thae's the takens I gie thee,
Nae doubt I will be there.

"They'll turn me in your arms, lady,
Into an esk and adder;
But hold me fast, and fear me now,
I am your bairn's father.

"They'll turn me to a bear sae grim,
And then a lion bold;
But hold me fast, and fear me not,
As ye shall love your child.

"Again they'll turn me in your arms
To a red-het gaud of airn;
But hold me fast, and fear me not,
I'll do to you nae harm.

"And last they'll turn me in your arms
Into the burning gleed;
Then throw me into well water,
O throw me in wi' speed.

"And then I'll be your ain true-love,
I'll turn a naked knight;
Then cover me wi' your green mantle,
And cover me out o' sight."

Gloomy, gloomy was the night,
And eerie was the way,
As fair Jenny in her green mantle
To Miles Cross she did gae.

About the middle o' the night,
She heard the bridles ring;
This lady was as glad at that
As any earthly thing.

First she let the black pass by,
And syne she let the brown;
But quickly she ran to the milk-white steed,
And pu'd the rider down.

Sae weel she minded whae he did say,
And young Tam Lin did win;
Syne covered him wi' her green mantle,
As blythe's a bird in spring.

Out then spak the Queen o' Fairies,
Out of a bush o' broom:

"Them that has gotten young Tam Lin
Has gotten a stately groom."

Out then spak the Queen o' Fairies,
And an angry woman was she:
"Shame betide her ill-far'd face,
And an ill death may she die,
For she's ta'en awa' the bonniest knight
In a' my companie.

"But had I kend, Tam Lin," she says,
"What now this night I see,
I wad hae ta'en out thy twa grey een,
And put in twa een o' tree."

[*nell*, keen, sharp, biting cold; *tiend*, forfeit; an, if; *mirk*, dark; *syne*,
next; *gaud*, goad (pointed bar used as a cattle-prod);
gleed, red-hot ember; *een*, eyes]

THE WASHER BY THE FORD

The fairy with the closest association with real human
death, rather than supernatural kidnap, is the *beansídhe*,
the banshee, the "woman of the hill." This priestess of the
dead was like a guardian spirit, attached to a particular
family or clan. The wailing and weeping of a beansídhe
signaled a forthcoming death. In the Highlands of
Scotland, her ominous presence might be glimpsed by a
stream, washing the bloodstained clothes of someone about
to die. Here she was known as the Washer
by the Ford.

DIVINE HAGS

The weird sisters, hand in hand,
Posters of the sea and land,
Thus do go about, about;
Thrice to thine, and thrice to mine,
And thrice again, to make up nine …
(CHANT OF THE THREE WITCHES IN *MACBETH*,
ACT 1, SCENE 3, WILLIAM SHAKESPEARE)

At Samhain, as the night of the year begins and the Moon becomes Queen of the Darkness, witches are abroad in force, raising the power in various ways to set the New Year off to a flying start. After dark, these half-human, half-supernatural beings may be seen cutting through the air on broomsticks or shank-banes (leg-bones), sailing in sieves or egg shells, or galloping along on cats transformed into horses, on their way to the Hallowmas Rade. Their favorite meeting places are lonely moors, deserted seashores, or churchyards, successors of the old burial mounds.

The stereotype of the witch—Shakespeare's "secret, black and midnight hag"—is indeed an awesome figure, for she is the village henwife or "cunning woman," with her secret knowingness, who has been cloned with the Dark-Moon Goddess, the Crone of Death, with her power of *wyrd*, or Fate. The expression "drawing down the Moon" is a further link: it was used to describe the magic rites of witches because they were thought to be worshipping the Moon.

The midnight hag, the mistress of fate, crops up in many different places—in old religion and magic, in poetry and story. Among the most terrifying of these hags was the third persona of the Irish Triple Goddess, the Morrígan, whose trinity was made up of the fertility goddess Ana, the mother Babd, and the crone Macha, "Queen of Phantoms". Sometimes—like mushroom spores quietly proliferating—the goddess's third death-hag aspect would multiply itself by three to become the sinister triad of Macha, Babd, and the Morrígan, known collectively as the Mórrígna. Whether in singular or plural form, the goddess's crone persona was a chilling figure who prophesied carnage and haunted battlefields, thirsting for blood. On his fateful journey to death, the Irish hero Cú Chulainn meets the Mórrígna on the road as "three Crones, blind of the left eye." After his end has been achieved, they perch on his shoulder in the form of crows.

Russian folklore has produced an equally frightful hag-witch—the infamous, human-flesh-eating Bába Yagá, who lives in a revolving hut that stands on chicken legs, and rides through the air in a giant mortar in pursuit of her victims. When the heroine Vasilísa first encounters her, she is terrified: "Next evening she came to the mead where Bába Yagá's hut stood. The fence round the hut consisted of human bones, and on the stakes skeletons glared out of their empty eyes. And instead of the doorways and the gate, there were feet, and in the stead of bolts there were hands, and instead of the lock there was a mouth with sharp teeth. And Vasilísa was stone-cold with fright…."

The Night-mare Life-in-Death was the specter conjured by the poet Samuel Coleridge in his epic poem *The Rime of the Ancient Mariner*. Aboard her skeletal ship, its "naked hulk" outlined against the setting sun, she dices with her sister, Death, for the life of the Ancient Mariner, guilty of the ultimate crime of shooting the albatross, the bird "that made the breeze to blow." She wins and thus consigns the Mariner to a living death on his becalmed vessel. The description of this particular death hag must be one of the most chilling in all literature:

> Her lips were red, her looks were free,
> Her locks were yellow as gold:
> Her skin was white as leprosy,
> The Night-mare Life-in-Death was she,
> Who thicks man's blood with cold.

OVERLEAF: The Night-mare Life-in-Death in her moment of triumph: she has defeated Death in a game of dice, and so won for herself the life of the Ancient Mariner.

One of the most famous English witches was Mother Shipton, who had tellingly divine powers including, of course, the ability to determine destiny. In an encounter with a local king, she told him to take "seven long strides" forward and, if he could then see the village of Long Compton, he would become King of England. As he took his last step, however, a mound sprang up, obscuring his view, whereupon the good Mother told him what his real fate would be:

> As Long Compton thou canst not see,
> King of England thou shalt not be.
> Rise up, stick, and stand still, stone,
> For King of England thou shalt be none,
> Thou and thy men hoar stones shall be,
> And I myself an eldern tree.

In the place where these words were uttered, the king and his army stand to this day, as frozen, petrified relics at the Neolithic burial site known as the Rollright Stones in the English Midlands—where perhaps they are still watched over by that emblem of witches, the elder tree.

A RALLYING CRY

At Samhain, witches were roused to action by rallying songs, such as this traditional one from Galloway, of which the following is a fragment:

> When the grey owlet has three times hooed,
> When the grimy cat has three times mewed,
> When the tod has yowled three times i' the wud
> At the reid mune co'erin ahint the clud,
> When the stars has cruppen deep i' the drift,
> Lest cantrips pyke them out o' the lift,
> Up, horses a', but mair adowe!
> Ryde, ryde for Lochar-brig-knowe!

[*tod*, fox; *wud*, wood; *reid mune*, red moon; *co'erin*, cowering; *ahint*, behind; *cruppen*, crept; *cantrips*, trickeries, spells; *pyke*, pick; *lift*, sky; *but mair adowe*, with more ado]

THE WITCH'S CAULDRON

Double, double toil and trouble;
Fire burn and cauldron bubble.
(CHORUS OF THE THREE WITCHES IN *MACBETH*,
ACT 4, SCENE 1, WILLIAM SHAKESPEARE)

The huge pot that was the witches' container of magic was an enduring and widespread pagan symbol of the Source of All Things, and had powerful connotations of the deep world-womb of the Great Mother, out of which life and wisdom came. In Greek myth, for example, the sorceress Medea resurrected King Aeson by boiling him in her cauldron, in the same fashion as Demeter restored life to Pelops.

Further north, the Celts had their own magical Cauldron of Regeneration. In Britain, it was brought as part of her wedding gift by Branwen the Beautiful when she married Matholwch, King of Ireland; plunged into this vat of resuscitation, dead men would rise again the following day (but would not have the power of speech). The Welsh bard Taliesin acquired his knowingness when he drank from the fount of wisdom that belonged to his mother, the goddess Cerridwen. Across the water, Irish Celts worshipped Badb, the One Who Boils, the middle persona of the triple Morrígan, who served up helpings of Life, Wisdom, Inspiration and Enlightenment.

Male deities had their cauldrons, too. The great stewpot of the Dagda, chieftain-god of the Irish Celts, always satisfied those who ate from it, and never emptied. In Scandinavia, Odin became the god of poetry after drinking the *hydromel*, the "mead of the poets" that was stored in two pitchers and in the cauldron Odrerir. First concocted by two dwarves from human blood and honey, this nectar of

The title page from a Wiccan book entitled The Shadow of the Golden Fire, *dated 1940. Wicca is a new form of religion, said to be a revival of pre-Christian paganism. This book belongs to the Gardnerian strand of Wicca, based on the ideas of Gerald Gardner.*

inspiration was later surrendered to the giant Suttung, who kept it in an underground chamber guarded by his daughter Gunnlöd. With cunning and trickery, Odin managed to gain the confidence of Suttung and the love of Gunnlöd—and thereby access to the hydromel, which he stole and carried off to his abode in the heavenly Asgard.

The pagan cauldron even found its way into Christianity as the Holy Grail, the cup that held Christ's life-blood.

"Witches" being burnt, in a German broadsheet of 1555. During the Church's fevered persecution of so-called witches in the 16th and 17th centuries, many women were accused of having supernatural powers and of being in league with the Devil.

In the beginning was the Word …
(ST. JOHN, CHAPTER 1, VERSE 1)

DANCING UP THE POWER

Twirling and whirling around in a dancing circle was another way to raise the power. As they danced, the witches sang. The North Berwick witches, in their trial before King James VI of Scotland in 1590, said that they had "danced entlang the kirkyaird, and Gelie Duncan playit on ane trump, Jhonne Fian missellit led the ring; Agnes Sampsoun and her dochteris and all the rest following … to the number of sevin scoir persounes," singing a song of which only the two following lines remain:

Cummer, gae ye afore,
cummer, gae ye;
Gif ye winna gae afore,
cummers, let me!

[*misselht*, muffled or masked; *dochteris*, daughters; *scoir*, score; *cummer*, a gossip ("gossip" originally meant "godparent"); *gif*, if.]

One of the chief agents witches use in their art is the Word—the rhyme, the chant, the name—all forms of spell. In Irish tales, the "spells of women" were known as *brichta ban*, and were much feared. In choosing this particular form of magic, witches are following an age-old tradition.

In the world of the Celts and Norsepeople, words had the power to charm and those who were expert in their use—the great poets—were priests and magicians, and were ranked with kings. In Wales, the master-poets were the bards; in Scandinavia, they were the skalds; in Ireland, they were the *ollamhs* who had to train for twelve years and pass through the "seven degrees of wisdom" before they could consider themselves qualified.

Such was the power of these wordwrights that it was most unwise to offend them, especially the Irish ones. An affronted Irish poet could compose an *aer*, a satire or cursing poem, that would bring out blotches or boils on his victim's face, turn his bowels to water, or drive him mad. Satires could also be used to blight crops or dry up milk, or for more practical purposes. On discovering that rats had eaten his dinner, the seventh-century *ollamh* Seanchan Torpest, uttered the insulting *aer*, "Rats have sharp snouts, yet are poor fighters"—whereupon ten of the insolent creatures fell dead on the spot.

O! well done! I commend your pains,
And every one shall share i' the gains.
And now about the cauldron sing,
Like elves and fairies in a ring,
Enchanting all that you put in.'

(HECATE, QUEEN OF THE WITCHES, IN
MACBETH, ACT 4, SCENE 1, WILLIAM
SHAKESPEARE)

The triple-headed Greek goddess Hecate. Guardian of three-way crossroads, she was also Hecate Trevia, Hecate of the Three Ways. Focusing on her Crone aspect, Christians of the Middle Ages named her Queen of the Witches.

HOW TO LIFT A WITCH'S SPELL

The only way to break a spell was with another magic charm:

A remedy for those bewitched. Take two horseshoes, heat them red hot, and nail one on the threshold of the door, but Quench the other in the Urine of the party bewitched: then set the urine over the fire in a pot or pipkin, and put the horseshoe into it. Make the urine boil, with a little salt put unto it, and three horseshoe nails, until it is almost all consumed: what is not boiled away, cast into the fire. Keep then your horseshoes and nails in a clean paper or cloth, and use the same manner three times. It will be the more effectual if it be done the change or full of the Moon.

(DOCTOR LILLY'S LAST LEGACY, 1683)

IN THE TWILIGHT
OF THE YEAR
THE RITES OF SAMHAIN

The wheel is come full circle ...
(*KING LEAR*, ACT 5, SCENE 3, WILLIAM SHAKESPEARE)

Samhain was attended by various rites and customs appropriate to the end of an Old Year and the beginning of a New—divinations, disguises, and, above all, bonfires. As a fire festival, Samhain equaled Beltane in importance: these were the two great fire festivals of the seasonal, lunar-based calendar, as Midwinter and midsummer were in the solar calendar.

Fire has always been sacred and magical—in Greek legend, it belonged to the gods and was stolen for mankind by Prometheus (in punishment for such a grave crime, the gods devised an exquisite torture: Prometheus, chained to a rock, should have his liver eaten by an eagle, and however much was devoured during the day would grow again during the night, to feed the winged monster once more). The power of fire might be used to mimic its parent, the Sun, or to cleanse, purify, and protect. Since the Celtic calendar is not solar-based it would seem that the prime purpose of the Samhain bonfire was the latter one—to repel and destroy any malevolent powers at this darkest point of the year, in much the same way as a fire might be lit to keep wild beasts at bay during the night. While the Beltane bonfires were kindled at dawn, those of Samhain were lit at dusk.

Fire, a sacred element, once belonged only to the gods. Its magical power can be used as an energizing force, or for purification.

Burning effigies on these ritual fires strengthened their magical effect. The effigy symbolized the harmful presence that required destruction, hence burning its image on the fire destroyed it, too. Effigies were relics of an earlier practice of using live victims, both human and animal. A Halloween custom from northeastern Scotland, that survived until comparatively recent times, hints at these dark origins. When the bonfire was in full flame, one boy would lie down as close to it as possible and the others would leap over him, in a wild, vaulting dance.

Another gruesome suggestion of Samhain sacrifice may be found in what is known as the Mythological Cycle of Ireland, recorded in the *Lebor Gabála Érann*, that melting pot of ancient Irish myth and history. Every year, on November 1, the people of Nemed were forced to supply to their demonic oppressors, the Fomoire, two-thirds of their corn, their milk, and their children. Such a toll may derive from memories of real and substantial offerings of agricultural produce and human sacrifice at this time—after all, Samhain was the gateway into the insecurity of Winter, when it was more important than ever to appease the forces of the supernatural.

A tradition persisted in Wales up to the early years of the twentieth century that also implies that bonfires once had a sacrificial use. Waiting until the last spark was out, those around the fire would suddenly take to their heels, shouting, "The cropped black sow seize the hindmost!" (The sow is the emblem of the Death Goddess in several mythologies). In other words, run for your life, or you may be caught and sacrificed. In Scotland, the pursuer suffered a gender change, and the cry became, "The de'il tak' the hindmost!"

THE NEW FLAME

Ancient Irish pagans knew the great power of the sacred flame. Every year, at Samhain, it is said, they kindled a new fire, from whose blessed flames all the other fires in Ireland were relit. Being the Celtic New Year, Samhain was the most efficacious time for this ritual, for the fire's magical influence could then last through the whole of Winter and Spring, to be recharged at Beltane.

Burn the Witch

Ge's a peat to burn the witches.

The effigy set alight in the Halloween bonfire was sometimes known as "the witch," and, in Scotland, boys going from house to house begging for peat to fuel the flames made it quite clear who would be symbolically consumed in them. The tradition of "burning the witch" is said to be of very great antiquity, being practiced even in ancient Babylon. In Scotland, where Halloween rites have been observed since time immemorial, it has survived from druidic times.

Several different streams of thought have fed the image of the witch—or the person believed to be a witch—as someone villainous and evil. The witch figure was, of course, a convenient target for people's fears, for she was credited with amazing abilities. She was thought to have power over the fertility of crops, animals, and humans; she could turn water into wine or milk; she controlled the weather, and could raise wind, hail and storm at will. With such supposed supernatural abilities at her command, the witch, it was believed, could influence the entire fortunes of the community for good or ill, as she chose. If the community were in good health, if crops and cattle had prospered, all was well; if calamity and disaster struck, however, the fault could conveniently be laid at her door. Having a scapegoat whom they could identify as the instigator of all their misfortunes—and whom they could then destroy by burning—restored the community's sense of order and security, and gave them a perception of control of their destiny.

> ## Fires on the Hillsides
>
> On the last day of autumn children gathered ferns, tar-barrels, the long thin stalks called *gàinisg*, and everything suitable for a bonfire. These were placed in a heap on some eminence near the house, and in the evening set fire to. The fires were called *Samhnagen*. There was one for each house, and it was an object of ambition who should have the biggest. Whole districts were brilliant with bonfires, and their glare across a Highland loch, and from many eminences, formed an exceedingly picturesque scene.
>
> (*The Golden Bough*, James Frazer, 1922)

Female witches, rather than their male counterparts, were the ones who came in for most abuse. Such persecution reflects a basic fear of women, and, in primitive times, man had good reason for such a fear. In the dawn of prehistory, when the role of the male in procreation was not understood, giving birth—producing another live human

being—was seen as the ultimate act of magic. Since only women were capable of this wonder, they clearly had innate knowledge of the great mysteries, which was denied to men. Like members of some secret magic circle, they were to be revered and respected. To them belonged the ultimate power—the power that brought men forth—and as women, the dominant sex, they stood in direct line of descent from the Great Mother herself, the progenitor of all.

Fear of the female and her secrets may be found in the later expression of pagan religion. In classical Greece, a new kind of paganism arose which may be called Apollonian, after the Greek Sun god, Apollo. This looked towards clarity, not mystery; towards the rational and not the inexplicable; towards the rites of the Sun. It stood in direct contrast to the older Dionysian religion with its ecstatic visions, and its dreamy, shadowy, shamanistic rites of the Moon. As the newer, patriarchal view took hold, the Old Religion was pushed to the sidelines and along with it witchcraft, with which it was associated: such a polarization still influences our attitudes.

If the witch's divine genes come from the mystical Goddess, her human genes are inherited from the real old woman, perhaps widowed or never married, who lived on her own at the edge of the village, and who had a knowledge of herbs and cures. Being outside the mainstream of the community, such a person became an object of suspicion, arousing feelings of fear and hostility—primitive tribal reactions to anyone who dares to differ and is therefore beyond the understanding of the limited imagination of the crowd.

All these strands of thought have fused together to give us the wicked witch and the wicked stepmother; they have also fueled Christian misogyny and the hysteria surrounding women accused of *maleficium*, evil-doing. When Christianity identified witchcraft as a specific—and rival—cult, it classified its adherents as heretics, its deities as demons. To rid the world of these opponents to the True Faith, the Church chose the pagan method of ritual purification by fire: thousands of supposed witches were burnt at the stake.

Like water seeping up from an underground well, the old ways will out, however: the custom of burning an alleged malefactor at the stake continues in England to this

OPPOSITE: The traditional English Bonfire Night falls five days after Samhain. It is celebrated with fireworks and a bonfire, on which an effigy of the historical character Guy Fawkes, known as the "guy," is sometimes burnt.

THE NEED FIRE

The ancestor of the great festival bonfires is the "need fire"—literally a magical fire created whenever the need arose. Also known as "wild fires" or "living fires," these fiery rites were usually performed to stem an outbreak of cattle disease, caused by evil spirits—proof of their antiquity for they date from the time when mankind survived on the products of their herds, rather than as farmers. Before a need fire could be lit, it was often necessary to put out all other fires and lights in the neighborhood, and the flame should not be struck with flint and steel, but by the friction of oak, the sacred wood.

day when, on November 5—halfway between Halloween New Style and Halloween Old Style—an effigy is ceremonially burnt in a bonfire. The figure consigned to the flames is supposedly that of the Roman Catholic Guy Fawkes who plotted to blow up the Houses of Parliament, and King James I with them, when the monarch came to open Parliament on November 5, 1605. His plan, known as the Gunpowder Plot, was leaked to the authorities, and thwarted. He and his accomplices were killed outright or savagely executed after being tried. Anyone who has been to the Guy Fawkes celebration with its wild bonfire, blackening effigy, and fireworks piercing the night sky-—all supposedly in memory of the saving of the realm—quickly sniffs the scent of ancient magic in the air.

BLAMING THE WITCHES

The fables of Witchcraft have taken so fast hold and deep rooted in the heart of man, that if any adversity, grief, sickness, loss of children, corn, cattle or liberty happen unto them, by and by they exclaim upon witches.

(THE DISCOVERY OF WITCHCRAFT, REGINALD SCOT, 1584)

THE GUISERS

As witches add their presence to the uncanny crowd abroad at Halloween, it is wise to take extra precautions for one's own safety. A particular threat may come from the throng of the returning dead, who may bear one away with them to the netherworld. In Mexico, for example, people who are away from home at this time try to return before the ghosts begin arriving so as to avoid meeting any of them along the lonely roads; falling asleep during their stay is also dangerous, for during sleep one's soul may be carried away. (This parallels the European custom of covering up any mirrors when someone in the house dies, in case the departing soul spots the reflections of the living in the glass, and bears them away for company in the afterlife.)

At the old druidic Samhain festival, those leading the rites wore masks to disguise themselves as spirits. Thus camouflaged, they were able to mingle with the real spirits of the dead who might otherwise recognize them and do them some mischief. This ancient custom passed into folk memory and the druidic

THE SHANDY DANN

The tradition of "burning the witch" was maintained at the castle of Balmoral in Scotland into the reign of Queen Victoria, where it was watched by the sovereign herself. The ceremony involved building an enormous bonfire, attended by clansmen in Highland garb, and the *Shandy Dann*, an effigy of a hideous old woman, so-called after the *shan-dre-dan*, the trolley from which she was hurled into the blaze, where she was burnt to ashes.

initiators became the Halloween *guisers*, people in disguise as ghouls, ghosts, witches, *urisks* (spirits of the forest) *kelpies* (spirits of the river), and more—the entire regiment of supernatural beings who roam the world at this season. Thus attired, the guisers would parade from house to house, singing and dancing.

Guising, and other Halloween customs, remained particularly strong in Scotland, but even there, its old significance was gradually eroded until it became no more than a bit of fun for children, wearing fancy dress and proclaiming "trick or treat."

The candles that were lit to illuminate the road from the grave are mimicked by the vegetable lanterns carried by the flesh-and-blood "ghosts" who troop the streets at Halloween. Such lanterns were once made using hollowed-out turnips.

Halloween lanterns may also be made from a thick cabbage stem which in Scotland produces what is known as a "kail-runt torch." Nowdays, of course, they are usually made from pumpkins, whose orange flesh glows like an ember of hellfire in the blackness of the night.

THE GUNPOWDER PLOT

Please to remember the fifth of November,
The gunpowder treason and plot.
I see no reason why gunpowder treason
Should ever be forgot.
'Twas God's mercy to be sent
To save our King and Parliament;
Three score barrels laid below,
For old England's overthrow
With a lighted candle, and a lighted match,
Boom, boom, to let him in.

(TRADITIONAL RHYME)

HALLOWEEN LANTERNS

Hallowe'en a nicht o' tine,
A can'le in a custock,
A howkit neep wi' glowerin' een
To fleg baith witch and warlock.
[Halloween a night of fire,
A candle in a cabbage stem,
A turnip lantern with glowing eyes,
To scare both witch and warlock.]

(TRADITIONAL SCOTS HALLOWEEN SONG)

OVERLEAF: Pumpkins make ideal Halloween lanterns. When lit from within, the ghoulish features cut in the side seem to glow with fire in the blackness of the night.

207

TRICKS

There is a whole repertoire of traditional pranks to choose from, once played by children in Halloween costume on their elders in imitation of the mischief-making Samhain spirits feared by our ancestors. Some are ingenious and must have had fairly dramatic effects, so are best not disclosed to modern children.... Here are two to sample:

Burning the reekie mehr Scoop out the center of a thick cabbage stem and fill it with *tow* (a kind of flax fiber, a wick); now you have your *mehr*, or taper. Light one end to make it *reekie*, or smoky, and apply to the keyhole of your chosen door. Blow through the unlit end and you will send a column of smoke into the house. When this loses its appeal, climb up on to the roof and block up the chimney with a piece of turf to prevent the smoke escaping; the interior will then become even more *reekie*.

Breaking glass This requires two pranksters, one of whom should be carrying a glass bottle. As one individual hits the window, the other immediately smashes the bottle against the wall, convincing those inside that the window has been broken.

TREATS

In the English county of Shropshire, children went from house to house singing the following song, and begging soul cakes or other goodies—rather like modern children with their "trick or treat":

Soul! soul! for a soul-cake!
I pray, good missis, a soul-cake!
An apple or pear, a plum or a cherry,
Any good thing to make us merry.
One for Peter, two for Paul,
Three for Him who made us all.
Up with the kettle, and down with the pan,
Give us good alms, and we'll be gone.

FORESEEING THE FUTURE

In the space that is Samhain, spanning the past and the future, one may look through the veil now thinned to almost glass-like transparency, and catch sight of the shape of things to come, waiting their turn to happen in the womb of future time.

Many of the divination rites of this most mystical period involved the use of foodstuffs, such as grains, vegetables, and fruit, as well as agricultural implements, showing that Halloween still had some lingering associations with the last of the harvest. The seasonal fires, too, provided a medium for foretelling the future.

Two of the most magically potent foods used in divination were the hazelnut and the apple. To the Celts, the hazel was the "magic tree that wizards love," containing "in a nutshell" all insight and wisdom. Gathering hazelnuts just before Halloween was a tradition on the Isle of Skye, off the coast of Scotland, where children would go to pick the nuts in a hazel grove beside a wishing well, thus—unknowingly perhaps—enacting one of the great legends of Celtic lore. These magic Nuts of Knowledge grew on the tree overhanging the Well of Enchantment in the Country-under-Wave. Every Samhain, the nuts ripened to scarlet and dropped from the bough, into the waiting mouth of the Salmon of Knowledge who then had understanding of "everything that passes, over-seas, and under-seas, and in hidden places and desert ways" and took this wisdom away with him as he swam "all the seas of the round and rolling world."

A HALLOWEEN SONG

The nicht is Hallowe'en and the
morn's Hallowday,
Gin ye want a true love, it's time
ye were away!
Tally on the window-brod,
Tally on the green,
Tally on the window-brod,
The nicht's Hallowe'en!

[*gin*, if; *tally*, from *tallywap*, to
give a blow or strike; *window-brod*, shutter]

(TRADITIONAL HALLOWEEN
RHYME OF THE GUISERS)

THE SILVER BOUGH

And the woman said unto the serpent, We may eat of the fruit of the trees of the garden:
But of the fruit of the tree which is in the midst of the garden, God hath said, Ye shall
not eat of it, neither shall ye touch it, lest ye die. And the serpent said unto the woman,
Ye shall not surely die: For God doth know that in the day ye eat thereof, then your eyes
shall be opened, and ye shall be as gods, knowing good and evil. And when the woman
saw that the tree was good for food, and that it was pleasant to the eyes, and a tree to be
desired to make one wise, she took of the fruit thereof, and did eat, and gave also unto
her husband with her; and he did eat. And the eyes of them both were opened …
(GENESIS, CHAPTER 3, VERSES 2-7)

THE GIFT OF PROPHECY

Thomas the Rhymer, the thirteenth-century English rhyming prophet, is said to have acquired his gift of foresight—his "tongue that could not lie"—from the Queen of Elfland herself. Enamored of Thomas, the Queen bore him off to her realm where she kept him for seven years, until the *teind*, the tribute that the fairies paid to the Devil, became due. Fearing that Thomas might be it, she returned him to the world of man, bestowing on him his telling tongue. As in the druidic Ordeal by Water, *The Ballad of True Thomas* tells how Thomas, after meeting the Queen at the Eildon Tree, and passing through her elfin hill, travels with her "by noise of flood" to the Land of Faerie. It was here that the Queen gave him the magic fruit of prophecy:

O they rade on, and further on,
And they waded thro' rivers abune
the knee.
Syne they cam to a gairden green,
And she pu'd an aipple frae a tree;
Tak this for thy wage, True Thomas,
she said,
It will gi'e thee tongue that ne'er can lee.

The magic groves of paganism shimmer with trees of gold and silver, for here flourish the mistletoe, sacred druidic plant and Golden Bough of ancient Greece and Rome, and the apple tree, the blessed Silver Bough of the Celts. Of all fruits, the apple is the most magical. It is the food that confers eternal youth and immortality on the gods, and any person fortunate enough to gain possession of a sacred apple will have access to the Otherworld, and be able to foresee the future.

Two of the traditional Halloween games that use the fruit of the apple tree are relics of old druidic divination rites. Perhaps the best known is apple bobbing, in which a number of apples are floated in a large tub of water. The water is stirred with a stick or some other equivalent of a druidic wand to keep the fruit in constant motion. As the apples bob along on the surface, each player has to try to pick one up using only his or her teeth. If successful, the player may then eat the apple—and thus acquire the power of foresight?

Popping hazelnuts by the fire on All Hallows' Eve was one way of looking into the future.

The druidic apple rite from which this derives is known as Ordeal by Water. Going through water to obtain apples symbolized the voyage to Avalon, "Apple Land," the magic island where gods and heroes lived, and where grew the fruits that gave the gift of knowingness to any who ate them.

The other main apple rite was Ordeal by Fire. In the modern equivalent, a small wooden rod is suspended horizontally at its center point from the ceiling; at one end is fixed a lighted candle or fir cone, and at the other an apple. The rod is set spinning, and each player in turn has to leap up and try to bite the apple without using hands, and without singeing the hair. Often the element of fire is left out, and only the apple swings from the ceiling.

NUTS AND APPLES

Halloween customs that offered a glimpse of the future were many and varied. Here are just two that predict how affairs of the heart will go:

• As the "witching hour" of midnight approaches, take a lighted candle and an apple, and go alone to a mirror in a darkened room. While eating the apple and combing your hair all the while, look into the mirror, and the face of your lover—or the Devil—will appear over your shoulder.

• Take two hazel nuts, or a pair of apple pips or grains of corn, and place them near a fire or on a hot ember or shovel. If you are Welsh and both nuts "pop and fly" at the same time, you will marry the object of your affections—but if they explode at different times you will part. If you are Scots, and the nuts burn quietly together, so will your passion, but if they spring apart, the same fate awaits you. If you are English, heed this rhyme:

If he loves me, pop and fly
If he hates me, lie and die.

THE STAR OF KNOWLEDGE

When an apple is cut horizontally (rather than from stalk to base), its pips reveal a pentacle pattern, called by Gypsies the "Star of Knowledge." The five-pointed apple-core pentacle was sacred to the Great Mother, survives in the Tarot pack in the Suit of Pentacles that is associated with the element Earth, and remains one of the prime emblems of witchcraft. In magic ritual, each of the four points at the sides represents one of the four elements, Water, Fire, Earth, and Air, while at the apex the fifth point represents Ether or quintessence—literally *quinta essentia*, the fifth essence or element. From this most subtle and pure substance the stars were formed, and it was this very essence of all matter that the alchemists sought to extract.

NOVEMBER'S CHILD

A child born at Hallowtide is sure to have second sight, and all November's children will be fortunate and beloved:

November's child is born to bless
He's like a song of thankfulness.

(TRADITIONAL RHYME)

READING THE STONES

Portents of the future might also be gleaned from the Halloween fire, in such matters, for example, as life expectancy:

• In one Scottish custom, the ashes of the Halloween fire were arranged in the form of a circle and a stone for every person in the families involved placed near the circumference. If one of the stones was displaced or damaged the following morning, the person whom it represented would die within the next year.

• In Wales, the great bonfire was known as *Coel Coeth*. When it had almost gone out, everyone, having marked a white stone to identify it, threw it into the dying embers. After saying their prayers around the fire, they went to bed. If any stone was missing in the morning, it was a sign that the person to whom it belonged would not live to see another Halloween.

WEATHER FORECAST

To know whether the Winter shall be cold or warm, go at Allhallows-tide to a Beech tree, and cut a chip thereof; if it be found Dry, then shall the Winter be warm.

(*THE SHEPHERD'S PROGNOSTICATION*, 1729)

The traditional Halloween game of catching an apple on a flaming rod. To win the sacred fruit, the players must endure trial by fire.

FULL CIRCLE

As the world reflects on what has gone before and gazes ahead to what is yet to be, Samhain is an appropriate time to say farewell, for the wheel has come full circle. As the Celtic twilight deepens, time moves out of the past and into the future, into yet another cycle of the seasons that—if Fate and the gods wish it—will bless mankind with health, happiness, and the very best of fortune. This traditional Welsh New Year carol expresses all our hopes for the promise of this new beginning:

> Here we bring new water
> From the well so clear,
> For to worship God with,
> This happy New Year.
> Sing levy-dew, sing levy-dew,
> The water and the wine;
> The seven bright gold wires
> And the bugles they do shine.
>
> Sing reign of Fair Maid,
> With gold upon her toe,
> Open you the West Door,
> And turn the Old Year go:
> Sing reign of Fair Maid,
> With gold upon her chin,
> Open you the East Door,
> And let the New Year in.

As the wheel of the year continues to turn the world looks forward to the birth of the new sun just before Beth, the Celtic tree month of the birch.

Pronunciation Guide

The following are approximate guides to the pronunciation of
Gaelic and Welsh words which appear in the book.
The letters "ch" are pronounced as in "loch" or "Bach."

GAELIC

FESTIVALS
Samhain	**Sow**-an
Imbolc	Im-**bole**
Beltane	**Bowl**-tan-a
Lughnasadh	**Loon**-as-sa

SUPERNATURAL BEINGS
Fomoire	Fo-**mor**-eh
leith bhrogan	let brog-**an**
Tuatha Dé Danann	**Too**-ah Day **Dan**-an
sidhe	shee
bean sidhe	**ban** shee
daoine sidhe	**deen**-ah shee

PLACES
Mag Tuireadh	Mag-**toor**-ah
Tir fo Thuinn	Teer fo Tonn
Tir na n'Oc	Teer na Noig

MYTHOLOGICAL CHARACTERS
Amairgen	A-**mar**-en
Balor	**Bail**-or

Cú Chulainn	Coo Cull-**en**
Dagda	Da-da
Diarmaid	**Deer**-mud
Dechtire	De-**teer**-ah
Fionn MacCumhaill	Fion Mac-**cool**
Gráinne	**Grawn**-ya
Lamfhada	**Lav**-fa-da
Lugh	Lug
Macha	Moch-**ah**
Mebd	Mev
Morrígan	**Mor**-eh-gawn
Mórrígna	**Mor**-eh-nya
Nuadu	New-**ah**-doo
Samildanach	Samil-**dawn**-och

MISCELLANEOUS
brichta ban	**bree**-ta ban
cailleach	**cal**-och
deiseil	**dee**-sail
gainisg	**gan**-iss
geasa	**gees**-ah
Lebor Gabála Érann	Low-er Gab-**bawl**-ah **Air**-ran

maidhdeanbuain	mad-en-**buane**
moilean Moire	moo-la Moy-reh
ollamh	**oal**-av
samhnagan	saun-ag-an
uschabheagh	ish-ka-**baa**-ha

Pwyll	Puyhl
Rhiannon	Hree-**ann**-on
Taliesen	**Tal**-yes-in
Teyron	**Ty**-ron

WELSH

MYTHOLOGICAL CHARACTERS

Afagddu	Av-**ag**-the
Arianrhod	Arr-ee-**an**-rod
Blodeuwedd	Blod-**eye**-weth
Cerridwen	**Kerid**-wen
Creiddylad	**Krythe**-il-ad
Greidawl	**Gray**-thawl
Gronw	**Gron**-oo
Gwion Bach	**Gwee**-on Bach
Gwyn ap Nudd	Gwin ap Neeth
Gwythr	Gwithr
Llew Llaw Gyffes	Hlew Hlaw **Guff**-ess
Llud Llawereint	Hleed Hlaw-**err**-aint
Matholwych	**Math**-oal-ooch
Pryderi	**Prid**-airy

MISCELLANEOUS

| coel coeth | coil coith |

BIBLIOGRAPHY

Bord, Janet and Colin, *Sacred Waters*, London, Granada, 1985.

Burland, C.A., *Echoes of Magic*, London, Peter Davies, 1972.

Campbell, Joseph, *The Masks of God: Occidental Mythology*, New York, Viking Penguin, 1964.

Crowley, Vivianne, *Wicca*, London, HarperCollins, 1989.

Eliade, Mercea, *Patterns in Comparative Religion*, trans. Rosemary Sheed, London, Sheed and Ward, 1958.

Eisler, Riane, *The Chalice and the Blade*, San Francisco, Harper & Row, 1987.

Encyclopedia of Magic and Superstition, London, Octopus Books, 1974.

Frazer, Sir James George, *The Golden Bough*, London, Macmillan, 1911-15.

Graves, Robert, *The White Goddess*, London, Faber & Faber, 1948.

Green, Marian, *A Calendar of Festivals*, Shaftesbury, Dorset, Element Books, 1991.

Hartland, Edwin Sidney, *The Science of Fairy Tales*, London, Methuen, 1925.

Kightly, Charles, *The Perpetual Almanack of Folklore*, London, Thames and Hudson, 1987.

Larousse Encyclopedia of Mythology, trans. Richard Aldington and Delano Ames, London, Paul Hamlyn, 1959.

MacCulloch, J.A., *The Religion of the Ancient Celts*, London, Constable, 1991.

Miles, Clement A., *Christmas in Ritual and Tradition, Christian and Pagan*, London, T. Fisher Unwin, 1912.

Miles, Rosalind, *The Women's History of the World*, London, Michael Joseph, 1988.

Newall, Venetia (ed), *The Witch Figure*, London, Routledge & Kegan Paul, 1973.

Rees, Alwyn and Brinley, *Celtic Heritage*, London, Thames and Hudson, 1961.

Pennick, Nigel, *The Pagan Source Book,* London, Random Century (Rider), 1992.

Walker, Barbara, *The Woman's Dictionary of Symbols and Sacred Objects,* San Francisco, Harper & Row, 1988.

The Woman's Encyclopedia of Myths and Secrets, San Francisco, Harper & Row, 1983.

Williamson, Robin, *The Craneskin Bag,* Edinburgh, Canongate, 1989.

Zimmer, Heinrich, *The King and the Corpse,* Bollingen Series XI, Princeton, New Jersey, Princeton University Press, 1948.

Essential Reading

Baring, Anne, and Cashford, Jules, *The Myth of the Goddess: Evolution of an Image,* Harmondsworth, Penguin Books (Viking), 1991.

Eliade, Mircea, *The Myth of the Eternal Return,* Bollingen Series XLVI, trans. William R. Trask, Princeton, New Jersey, Princeton University Press, 1971.

INDEX

Acknowledgments

TEXT ACKNOWLEDGMENTS

p. 101: Taliesen's greeting from *The Craneskin Bag* by Robin Williamson, reproduced with permission of Curtis Brown Ltd, London, on behalf of Robin Williamson. Copyright © Robin Williamson 1989.

p. 119: I danced in the morning (*Lord of the Dance*) by Sydney Carter. Copyright © 1963 Stainer & Bell Ltd. Reproduced by permission of Hope Publishing Company, Illinois 60188, for the USA and Canada, and Stainer & Bell Ltd, London, England, for the rest of the world.

pp. 136, 139: Excerpts from *The Stolen Child* and *The Land of Heart's Desire* by W. B. Yeats quoted with permission of A. P. Watt literary agents on behalf of Anne and Michael Yeats.

Every effort has been made to trace all present copyright holders of the material used in this book, whether companies or individuals. Any omission is unintentional and we will be pleased to correct any errors in future editions of this book.

PICTURE ACKNOWLEDGMENTS

AAA: 14

AKG LONDON: 36, 78, 91, 105, 175

ANN RONAN AT IMAGE SELECT: 16, 18, 19, 25, 34, 69, 124, 147, 182, 189

COLLECTIONS: Geoff Howard 35, Brian Shuel 170, 202

MARY EVANS: 62/63 72/73, 95, 123, 169, 211, 213

IMAGE SELECT: Novovitch Liaion 6, Raphael Gaillarde 144

IMAGES COLOUR LIBRARY: 4, 8, 9, 10/11, 12, 13, 15, 17, 18, 20, 22, 23, 25, 26/27, 32, 37, 38, 46, 52, 53, 55, 57, 58/59, 64, 71, 75, 77, 79, 81, 83, 87, 88, 92, 98/99, 103, 106/107, 109, 111, 114, 117, 118, 120, 125, 131, 133, 135, 137, 138, 143, 145, 150, 152, 155, 156, 157, 158, 189, 160/61, 162r, 162l, 167, 176/77, 179, 180, 190/91, 193, 194/95, 197, 199, 214, Title page.

TELEGRAPH COLOUR LIBRARY: 205, 206/7, 208

ZEFA: 24, 28, 39, 50, 67, 108